APPLE WATCH SENIORS GUIDE

The Step-by-Step Illustrated Manual for Seniors to Master their Apple Watch with Ease

2024

BONUS TIPS AND TRICKS!

AWARD WINNING GUIDE

- LARGE VIEW
- FULLY ILLUSTRATED
- EMERGENCY S.O.S. (911)
- HEART RATE NOTIFICATIONS
- WATER LOCK
- STEPS TRACKER

AND MUCH MORE...

BRAD JORDAN

TABLE OF CONTENTS

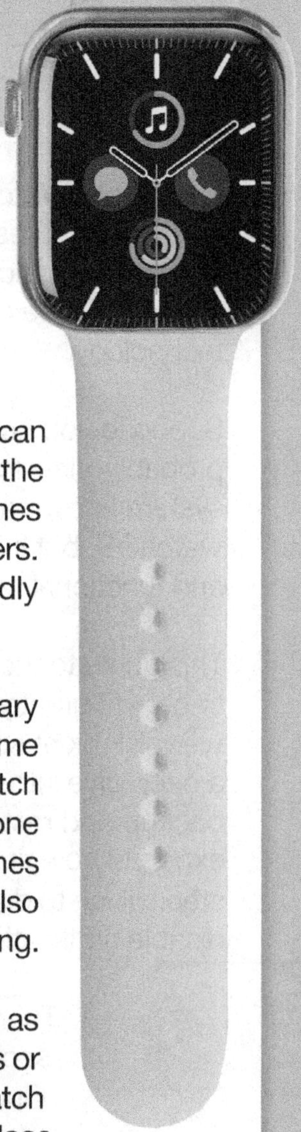

INTRODUCTION

Smartwatches are the most common type of wearable technology that you can don just like a regular watch. However, they can do far more than just tell the time. The **Apple Watch** is one of the most advanced and premium smartwatches available on the market, with its patented rectangle face and rounded corners. It integrates seamlessly with your **iPhone** or iPad to give you a user-friendly experience to help you live your healthiest and most productive life.

Most smartwatches are **Bluetooth-enabled devices**, and this is their primary means of communicating and syncing data with your **iPhone**, though some smartwatches do have cellular connectivity as well. Bluetooth enables the watch to act as an extension of your **iPhone** so that you can receive messages or phone calls, see your emails, listen to music, get directions, or use Siri. Smartwatches not only extend the functions of your phone directly to your wrist, but they also collect real-world data that you can use to improve and monitor your well-being.

Many smartwatches have touch screen displays that work in the same way as your phones, tablets, and iPads. They also feature a limited number of buttons or a crown so that you can navigate through the software with ease. A smartwatch has a strap just like a normal watch, either with a clasp or clip to keep it in place. You can often choose from various strap materials, such as the more rugged and sports-oriented silicon straps or a more refined and elegant metal strap.

Smartwatches like the **Apple Watch** are most commonly used as fitness tracking devices, and they can monitor your steps, heart rate, and calories burned, along with any relevant GPS data that you can use to view your running or walking routes and calculate your average pace and distance covered. The **Apple Watch** takes this approach many steps further with its advanced heart health features, blood oxygen level and sleep monitoring, and emergency functions like SOS calls and fall detection. The **Apple Watch**, along with a few other types of smartwatches, has adopted contactless payment functionality so that you can connect your bank card directly to your watch and tap it to pay for goods and services.

Smartwatches also allow you to interact with your social media and messaging apps by alerting you to notifications and responding to messages so that you can always stay in the loop and be in touch with those you care about.

The **Apple Watch** allows you to install a wide variety of apps directly from the App Store to meet any of these needs and so much more. You can download companion apps, which are versions specifically designed for your **Apple Watch** that work alongside the version **iPhone.** These companion apps often offer unique functions that take advantage of wearable technology.

Suppose you have chosen the **Apple Watch** as your preferred wearable. In that case, you are probably already familiar with the family of Apple products and the Apple mobile operating system known as iOS. The **Apple Watch** runs on very similar software to the **iPhones**, called watchOS, but it is more streamlined and simplified to accommodate the limited display size and functionality.

This guide to the **Apple Watch** is tailored especially for seniors and older adults who will stand to benefit greatly from the advanced health features that will be discussed in detail. But first, we will look at some of the different **Apple Watch** models and their differences, and then take a deep dive into some of the basics of using an **Apple Watch**, including how to set it up, pair it, backup and restore, and how to navigate using the buttons and controls. You will become an expert in now time and confidently manage all your custom settings and preferences. The next step will be to discuss some of the functions of your **Apple Watch**, including how to set up and disable notifications, select or create your own watch faces, and add even further functionality.

There are some important safety and security sections to look out for, such as how to activate Find My and protect your data if your device is lost or stolen. Finally, we learn about the health features and how they can protect you and alert you to any potential health risks, as well as a wide range of built-in and third-party apps that you can use.

Don't miss the **tips and tricks** at the end of the book, which can come in handy.

CHAPTER 1: Specifications

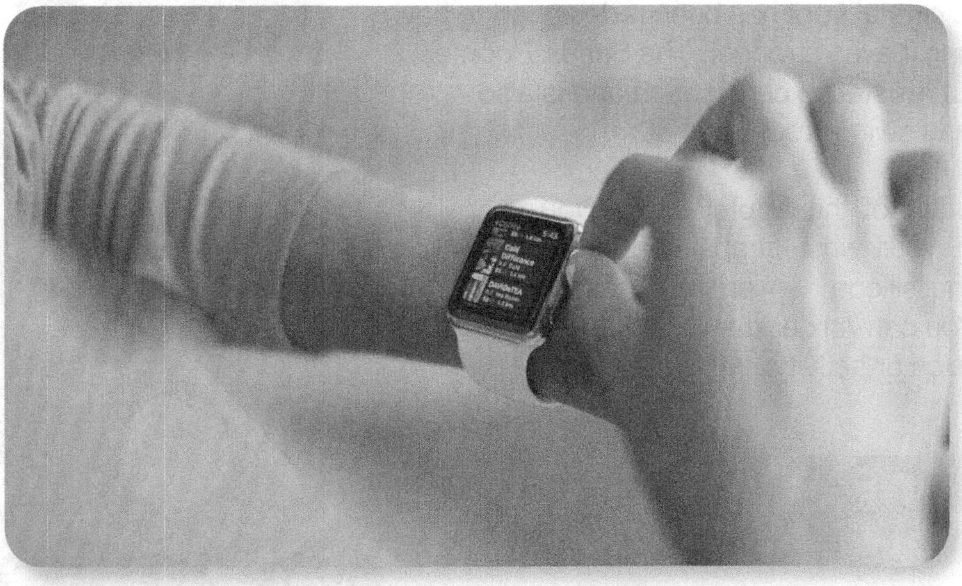

All of the **Apple Watches** have the same basic design. There is a square watch face with a digital retina display. Along the side of the watch face are the **Digital Crown** and the side button. You will see the heart rate sensor, microphone, and speaker on the back of the watch's face.

The Most Advanced Apple Watch Ever

The newest and most advanced model of the Apple Watch is the Series 7. It comes in either a 45mm or 41mm case size, and you can choose between a wide selection of colors and finishes: there are five new colors in the aluminum finish, three stainless steel options, two colors in titanium, as well as the unique Nike and Hermès models.

The Series 7 comes with the largest retina display of any model, with a 20% larger screen area than the next model in the line, the SE, and about 50% more screen area than the Series 3. It has an LTPO OLED always-on retina display with force touch. This means you get a much crisper display with more vivid colors; you can always see your essential information like date and time, and the watch can respond to your touch in many different ways. The Series 7 display has 396x484 pixels and a small border width of only 1.7mm. This is a large display compared to the SE and Series 3 models. The SE comes with 368x448 pixels and a 3.0mm border width, while the early Series 3 has only 312x390 pixels and a larger border width of 4.5mm.

The crack-resistant front crystal protects your display and is very durable, being about 50% thicker than in other models. The shape of the crystal front has been redesigned to have a flat base, making it even stronger. The Series 7 comes with an IP6X dust resistance certification and is also water-resistant and swim-proof up to 50m.

Like with all models of the **Apple Watch**, you can easily swap out your wrist straps for different designs, including silicon, woven fabrics, or even metal options. You can mix and match your straps to suit any occasion or activity.

The Series 7 also has an improved charging system to keep your **Apple Watch** running for longer and requires less time to charge fully. The Series 7 will be able to charge its battery about 33% faster than the previous Series 6, taking only 45 minutes to go from 0% to 80% and providing up to 18 hours of use time.

Some features you can find in all models of the **Apple Watch** include a speaker and a microphone, though the Series 7 and SE models have improved second-generation speaker units to improve sound quality. All models come with an altimeter to measure your height above sea level, though the Series 3 only works when you open the altimeter app, whereas the Series 7 and SE models are always on. The Series 6 and SE models also come with compasses to help you navigate and orient yourself. All models come with GPS functionality as well. The Series 7 and SE models have **Digital Crowns** with haptic feedback, which will respond to your touch with small vibrations, giving you a more tactile and intuitive experience. The processors that handle the computing in the **Apple Watch**es are all advanced and fast. However, improvements in each successive model continue to advance your user experience and reduce any delays.

Older Models

is not a Series 7 or SE, you can still get many benefits. There

If your **Apple Watch** is not a Series 7 or SE, you can still get many benefits. There are some critical health features that you may miss, such as the blood oxygen app, the ECG app, fall detection, noise monitoring, and international emergency calling.

Apple Watch Series and The Monitoring of Your Heart Health

The Series 7 also comes with some of the most advanced health features to help you track all your vitals. Only the Series 7 comes with blood oxygen and electrical heart sensors, but all have an optical heart sensor. However, the SE has a second-generation and the Series 7 has a third-generation optical heart sensor. It can measure heart rate and blood oxygen levels, helping you make sure you are absorbing oxygen into your body correctly. You can now take an electrocardiogram (ECG) at any time using your **Apple Watch**. With this information, you can take some control over your health and also support your doctors. The Series 7 can identify irregular heart rhythms, low heart rates, or high heart rates and alert you when necessary. This is just one of the many health-focused features that come standard in the Series 7 that you can take advantage of. These small changes and improvements make a big difference in the accuracy and value of the health readings you can expect.

The Series 7 and SE models have 4G LTE connectivity, Wi-Fi, and Bluetooth. The Series 3 only has Wi-Fi and Bluetooth. The 4G LTE connectivity allows you to stay connected with friends and family using your cellular connection when there is no access to a Wi-Fi network.

The Series 7 and SE models also improve your safety with several emergency features. Though all models have emergency SOS capabilities, allowing you to alert your emergency contacts quickly, only the Series 7 and SE models have international emergency calling, fall detection, and noise monitoring. These features will be discussed in the Health Focus chapter.

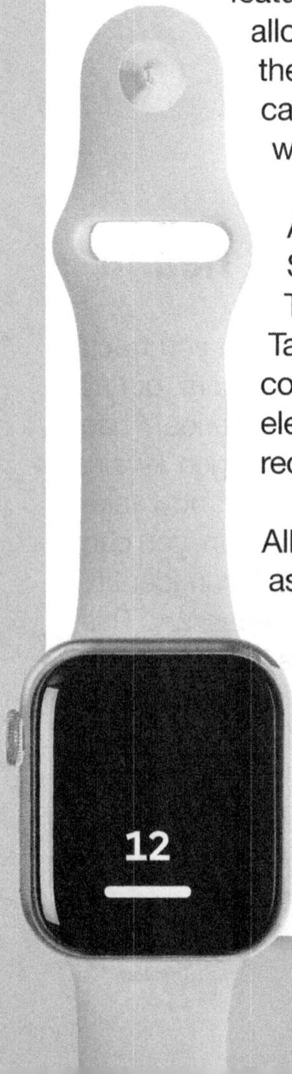

Along with all of these innovative health features, the Series 7 also boasts impressive environmental features. The cases are made from 100% recycled aluminum; the Taptic Engine uses 100% recycled tungsten; all magnet components are made from 100% recycled rare earth elements; and the tin in the SiP components is also 100% recycled.

All models are designed to be as energy-efficient as possible and come standard with responsible packaging that maximizes paper packaging, which is recyclable and reduces plastic use. All models have arsenic-free glass displays, and they are also free from mercury, BFRs, PVC, and beryllium toxicants.

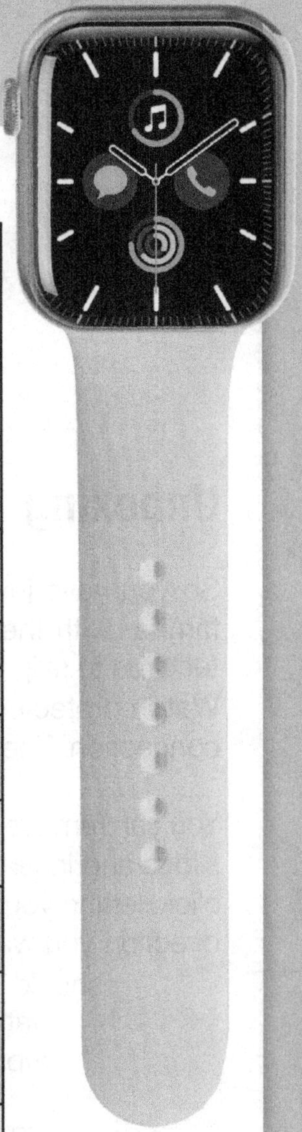

SERIES 7	SERIES SE	SERIES 3
45 mm or 41 mm case size	44 mm or 40 mm case size	42 mm or 38 mm case size
5 Different Aluminum Finishes & 3 Stainless Steel Finishes	3 Different Aluminum Finishes	2 Different Aluminum Finishes
LTPO OLED Always-On Retina display with Force Touch	LTPO OLED Retina display with Force Touch	Series 3: OLED Retina Display with Force Touch
Water Resistant and Swim Proof up to 50 m	Water Resistant and Swim Proof up to 50 m	Water Resistant and Swim Proof up to 50 m
Blood Oxygen App	Not available	Not available
ECG App	Not available	Not available
High and Low Heart Rate Notifications	High and Low Heart Rate Notifications	High and Low Heart Rate Notifications
Irregular Heart Rhythm Notifications	Irregular Heart Rhythm Notifications	Irregular Heart Rhythm Notifications
Third-generation optical heart sensor	Second-generation optical heart sensor	Optical heart sensor
Emergency SOS Calling	Emergency SOS Calling	Emergency SOS Calling
International Emergency Calling	International Emergency Calling	Not Available
Fall Detection	Fall Detection	Not Available
Noise Monitoring	Noise Monitoring	Not Available
Compass	Compass	Not Available
Always-On Altimeter	Always-On Altimeter	Altimeter
Cellular connectivity on GPS + Cellular models	Cellular connectivity on GPS + Cellular models	Not Available
GPS Enabled	GPS Enabled	GPS Enabled
Fast Charging	Not Available	Not Available
Second-Generation Speaker and Mic	Second-Generation Speaker and Mic	Speaker and Mic

CHAPTER 2: Getting Started

Unboxing

So you have just purchased your own **Apple Watch**, and now it's time to unbox it and get familiar with the design and interface. (If you have already started using your **Apple Watch**, feel free to skip to the next section). Upon opening the packaging, you will find your Apple **Watch** protected in a foam cover. You will also get a magnetic charging cable with a USB-C connection. The straps are provided separately.

You can remove your watch face from the foam cover and insert your straps by using the metal slides and inserting them into slots on the back of the watch face. You should hear and feel a click, letting you know that the straps have been inserted correctly. You can also choose which direction you want the clasps to face, and the watch can be worn on your right or left arm. It should be worn with the right - not too tight and not too loose. The back of the watch face needs to contact the skin for its features, like the heart rate sensor, to work properly.

The charging cable is very easy to use. Simply plug the USB-C into a power source and then place the back of the watch face onto the round surface. You will feel that it is held in place by magnets, and the watch should turn on or show an icon indicating that it is charging properly.

Never force your charging cables into their connectors, as the pins inside may bend or break. If you struggle to insert the cables properly, check for any obstructions or damage, and make sure you have matching components. Certain usage habits, like charging your device while you use it, can cause the cables to become damaged, frayed, or break. If you repeatedly bend your cables in the same spot through repetitive use, they will become weak and brittle and subject to breaking. Do not force the cables into sharp angles, and instead try to make sure that they can follow smooth curves. You should regularly inspect your cables and charging devices for any damage, breaks, or bends and discard them if you notice any problems.

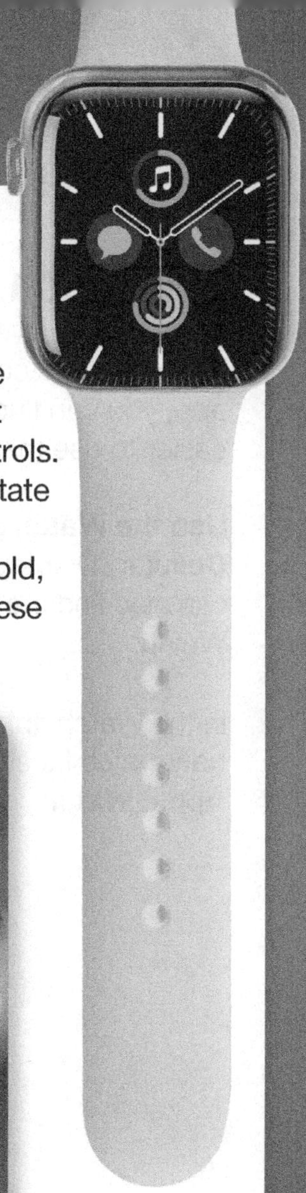

Buttons and Controls

On the side of your watch, you will find the Digital Crown and the side button. You will use these controls and the touch screen display to interact with your **Apple Watch.** You can use different actions with each of these controls. The **Digital Crown** allows you to press, press and hold, double-press, and rotate to carry out different actions. You can press, double-press, and hold the side button. The digital display uses various gestures, including tap, tap and hold, drag, swipe, and force touch. You can also use the 'glance' gestures. All of these actions will be discussed in a later section.

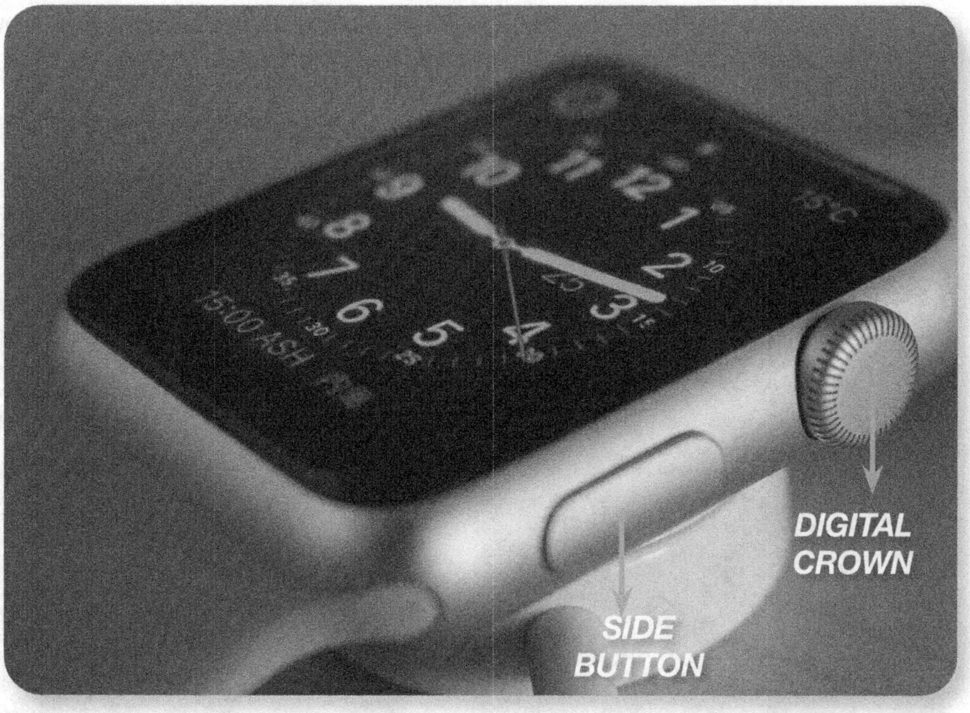

You will never need to use excessive pressure on the button, **Digital Crown**, or **Apple Watch** display to get a response. If your **Apple Watch** is unresponsive, there may be dirt that is causing the buttons to jam or obstruct the screen. Follow the cleaning instructions at the end of this title or contact your nearest Apple Service Provider for advice.

The Watch App

You will find a companion app for your Apple Watch installed on your iPhone. Through this app, you can find most settings and customization options for the APple Watch, and it is a lot easier to use than the Settings app on your Apple Watch itself.

Use the Watch app to access Notifications, App View, Dock settings, and your General, Cellular, Display & Brightness, Sounds & Haptics, Passcode, and Pricavy settings. You can also find the settings for each of the installed apps that are compatible with your Apple Watch.

In the Watch app, you can also access the Face Gallery, where you can browse and download new watch faces, and the App Store, where you can find new apps to get the most of your **Apple Watch**.

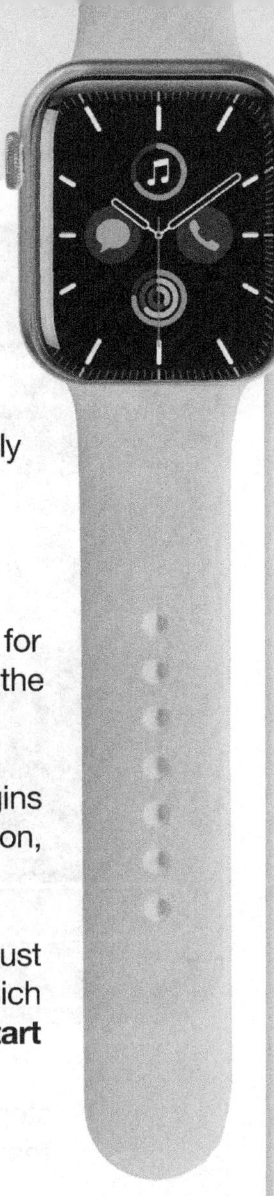

Pairing

Your Apple Watch must be paired with your iPhone.

1. The watch should be fitted onto your wrist with the straps appropriately fastened.

2. Make sure you have your iPhone with you.

3. Turn on your Apple Watch by pressing and holding the side button for a few seconds. You can let go when you see the Apple logo appear on the screen.

4. You should see an alert on your iPhone as the watch automatically begins to search for nearby devices. When you see the Apple Watch pairing option, you can select 'continue.'

5. If you do not see this alert, you must manually open the **Apple Watch** app, which is installed on your **iPhone**. Select **'Start Pairing'** to continue.

6. Choose **'Set Up for Myself'.**

7. Your **iPhone's** viewfinder will open so that you can scan the display of your **Apple Watch**. On your **Apple Watch** display, you will see an animation appear. Use your **iPhone** to scan the animation on your **Apple Watch** display.

8. You can choose to set up your **Apple Watch** as a new device. If you have had previous models of the **Apple Watch**, you can also choose to restore a backup that will sync all of your previous settings with the new model.

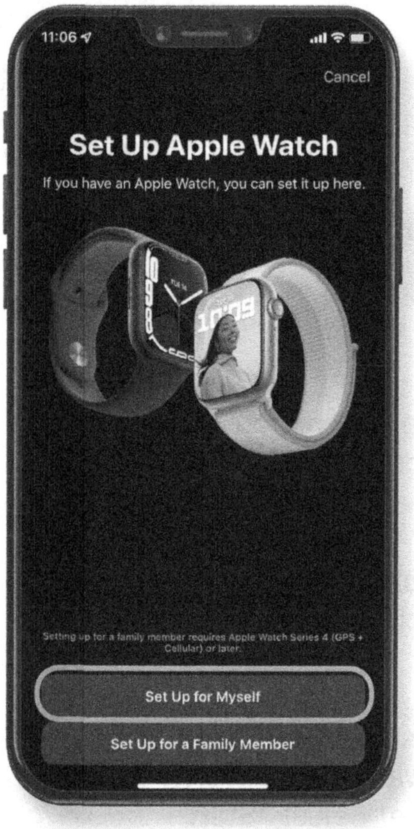

9. Once this is complete, select **'Set Up Apple Watch'** and simply follow the remaining setup steps. The app will ask you to set up a few different settings and select your preferences, such as the text size. Change the font size by dragging the slider across the screen, and enable or disable bold text using the toggle switch. You can change any of these selections later.

10. You will be asked to choose a passcode for your **Apple Watch**. Your passcode must be four numerical digits long, or you can choose to use a longer password instead. You can skip this step if you don't want a passcode, but it will be necessary if you want to use features like Apple Pay.

11. Next, your **Apple Watch** will begin installing any required software updates. You should keep automatic updates turned on to enable your **Apple Watch** to run the latest software.

12. One of the final requests you will see is the option to set up **Apple Pay** on your **Apple Watch**. Add your bank card details or choose to set this up later.

13. You will see some information about the Emergency SOS feature on the next screen. This feature allows you to get in touch with emergency services or your designated emergency contact by pressing and holding down the side button on your **Apple Watch**.

14. If you have a newer model of the **Apple Watch**, you will also see some information about the Always-on feature. This feature enables the display to be on at all times, rather than going into a sleep mode like older models. This uses slightly more battery power and can be disabled in the settings, though

it allows you to see the time without needing to use special gestures to wake up the display.

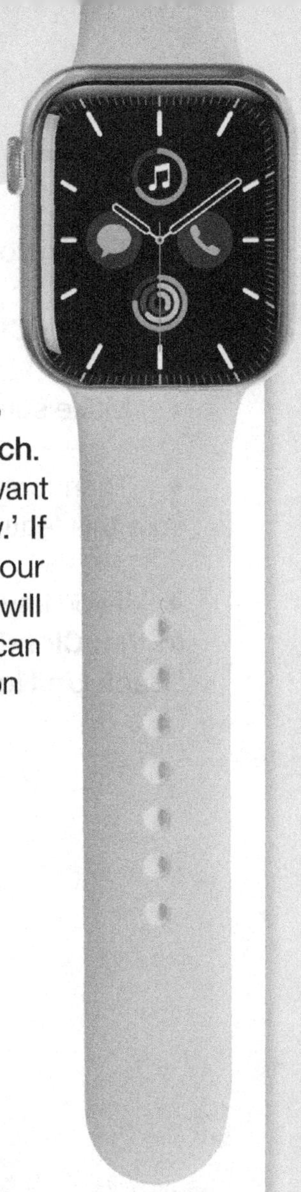

15. Finally, you will be prompted to select and install apps on your **Apple Watch.** First, select which type of view you want to use, either the 'grid view' or 'list view.' If you have companion apps installed on your **iPhone**, you can select them, and they will be installed on your **Apple Watch**. You can find companion apps on the App Store on your iPhone.

Backup and Restore

It's a good idea to make a backup of your **Apple Watch**. This allows you to restore your data if you need to reset your device or if you lose your device. The backup will be stored on your **iPhone** and can be accessed with your Apple ID. When you unpair your **Apple Watch** from your **iPhone**, it will automatically create a backup.

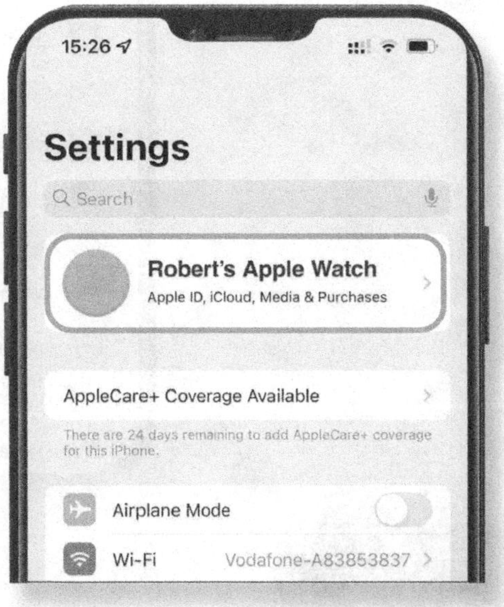

- Once paired, you can make sure that your **Apple Watch** is being backed up by checking your iCloud settings:

- On your **iPhone**, go to the **Settings app**.

- Tap on your **name** at the very top of the menu.
- Select **iCloud.**
- Make sure this feature is turned on.
- Then look for Watch in the list of apps, and make sure this feature is also toggled on.
- If you have not backed up your data recently, scroll to the **iCloud Backup option** and tap it. Then select **"Back Up Now".**

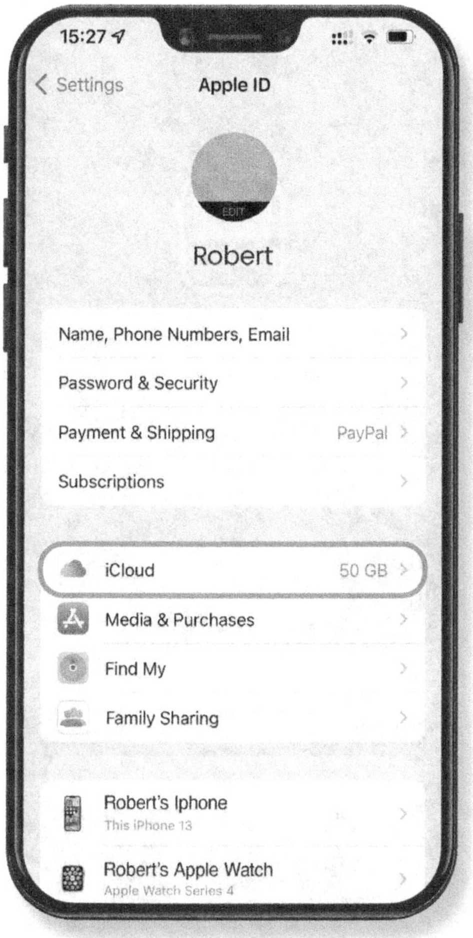

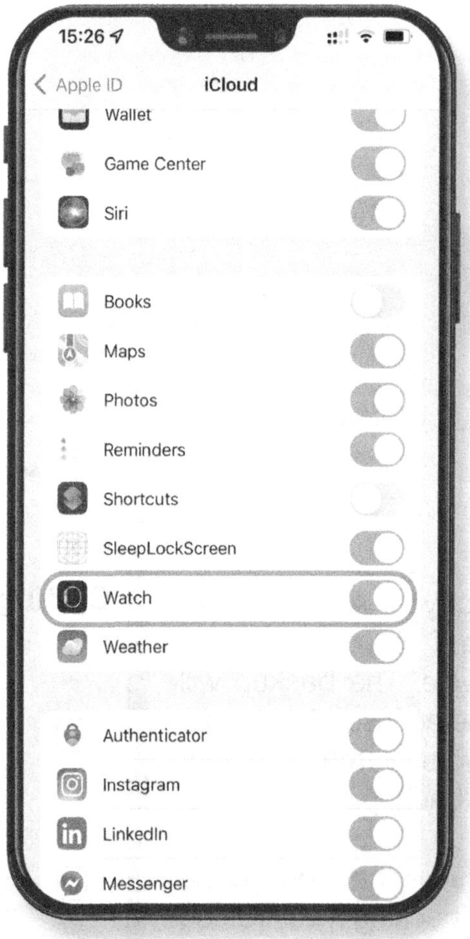

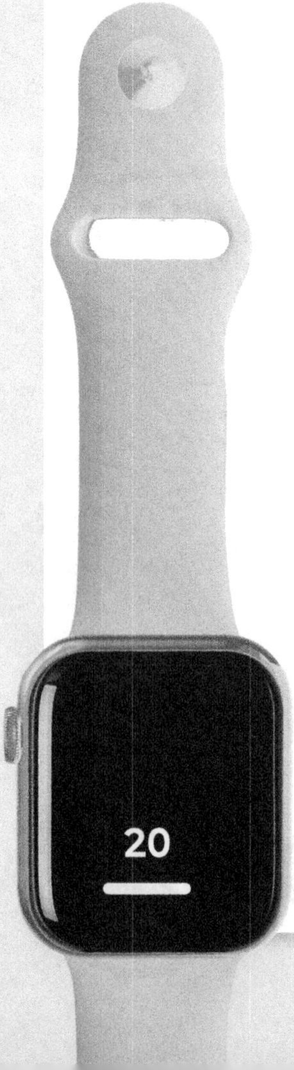

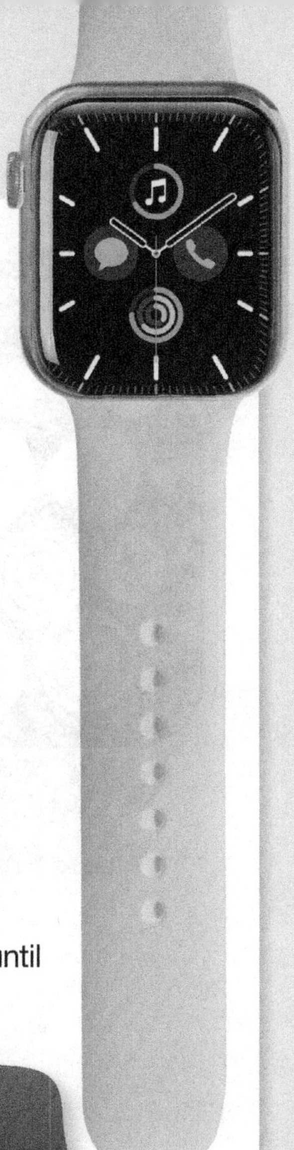

CHAPTER 3:

Getting Familiar with the Apple Watch

Basic Settings

Turning your Apple Watch ON or OFF:

- **Turn your Apple Watch ON** by pressing and holding the side button until you see the Apple logo appear on the screen.

- **Turn your Apple Watch OFF** by pressing and holding the side button until a menu appears. In the menu, you will see a **Power Off slider** and a **Medical ID** and **Emergency SOS** slider. Drag the power icon to the right to turn your **Apple Watch** off. You will not often have to turn your **Apple Watch** off; it will remain on for most of the time.

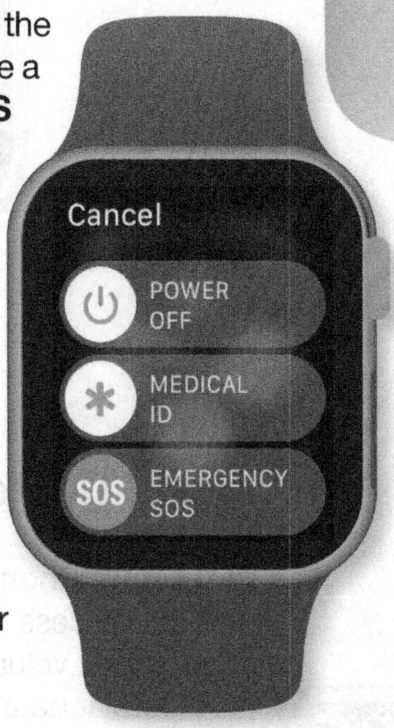

Waking your Apple Watch

- Your **Apple Watch** will automatically wake up when you raise your wrist, and it will go back into sleep mode when you lower your wrist. This makes the device very intuitive and easy to use.

- You can also wake your **Apple Watch** by pressing or turning the **Digital Crown** or by tapping on the display.

The Settings app

- You can access the **Settings app** by pressing the **Digital Crown**, which will open the Home Screen. From there, tap the gear icon to open the **Settings app**.

- In the **Settings app**, you can find several different settings such as **General, Display & Brightness, Sounds & Haptics, Passcode,** etc.

- Use your finger to scroll through these different settings.

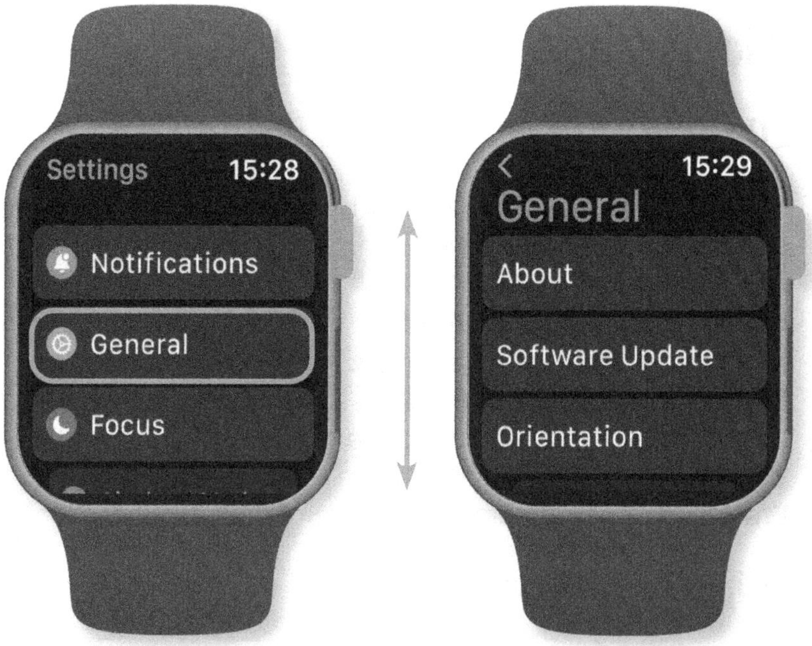

Control Center

Just like your **iPhone**, your **Apple Watch** has a **Control Center**. This menu gives you quick access to some of the most important settings and shortcuts, like brightness, volume, silent mode, sleep mode, flight mode, battery status, Wi-Fi, cellular data, and Bluetooth.

- You can only access the Control Center from the **Home Screen**. Press the **Digital Crown** to return to the Home Screen.

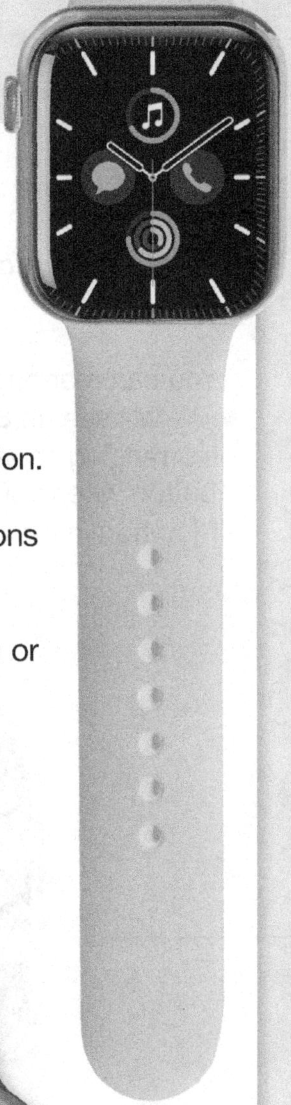

- Swipe upwards from the bottom of the screen to bring up the Control Center menu.
- You will see small icons showing you information or acting as shortcuts for different settings.
- Tap any of these icons to see more information.
- Swipe up or down to scroll through the icons in the Control Center.
- To close the Control Center, swipe down or press the **Digital Crown**.

Some of the available shortcuts you will find in the Control Center may include:

- **Cellular data** (turn on or off)
- **Wi-Fi** (turn on or off)
- **Ping your iPhone**
- **Battery** indicator
- **Silent mode** (turn on or off)
- **Lock** (turn on or off)
- **Theater mode** (turn on or off)
- **Walkie-Talkie** (turn on or off)
- **Focus/Do Not Disturb** (turn on or off)
- **Flashlight** (turn on or off)
- **Airplane mode** (turn on or off)
- **Water Lock** (turn on or off)

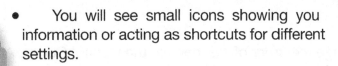

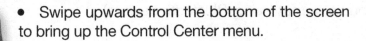

- **Choose audio output** (select Bluetooth devices)
- **Announce Notifications** (turn on or off)

You can rearrange the order of the icons in the Control Center. At the bottom of the icon list, you will see an **Edit button**. Tap this button, and the icons begin to shiver just as if you were rearranging shortcuts on your **iPhone**. Drag the icons to their new locations and tap the Done button when you are finished. You can also remove buttons that you do not use by hitting the [-] button in the corner of the icons.

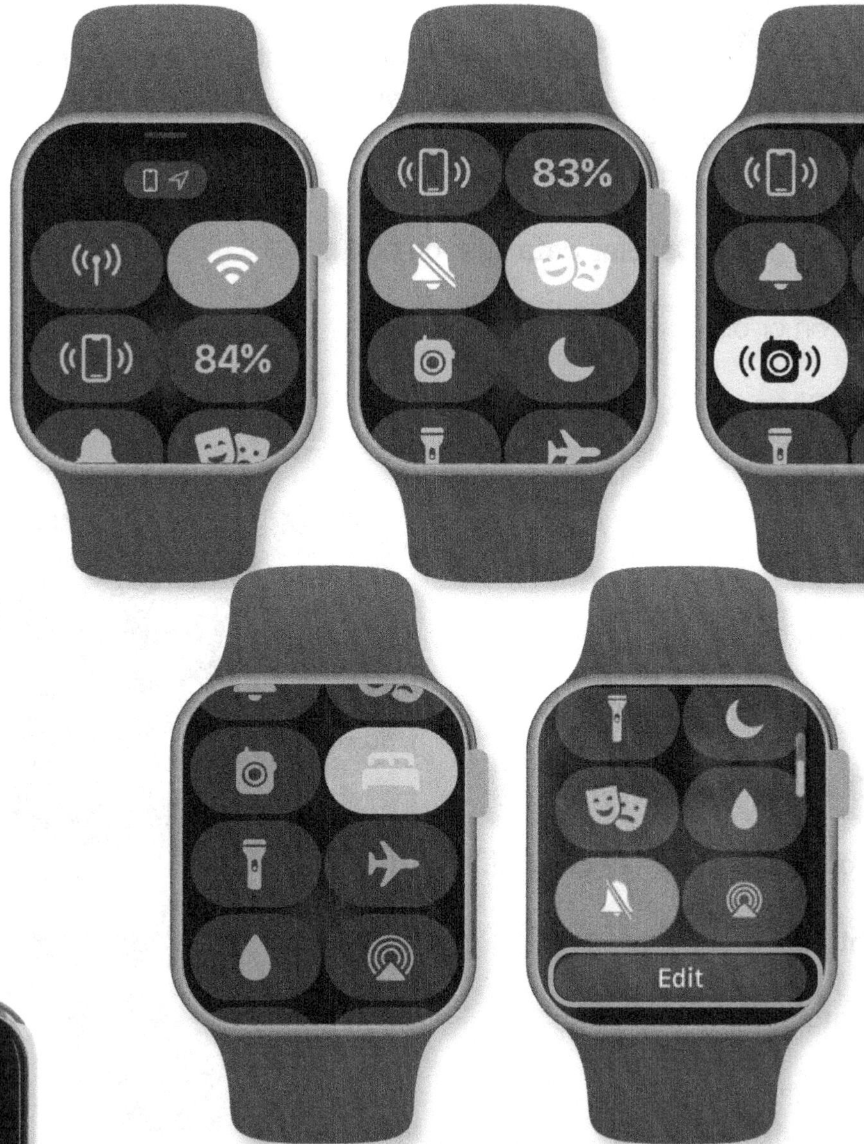

Click Edit to rearrange the icons

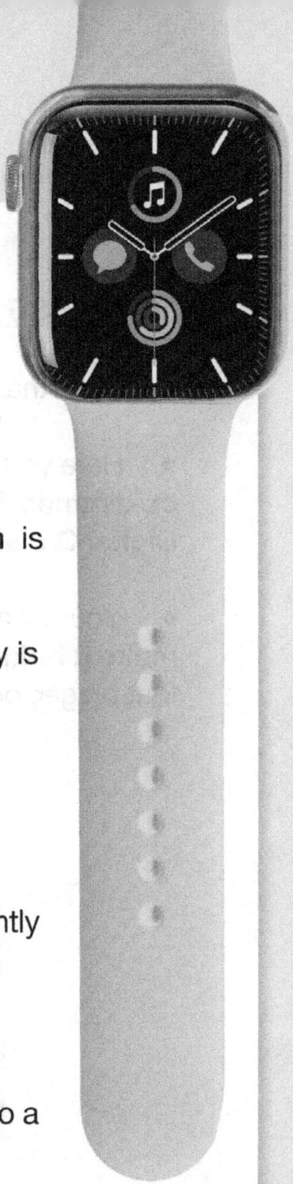

Status Icons

The screen on your **Apple Watch** is much smaller than on your **iPhone**, iPad, or Mac device, and so it relies on using small and simple icons to convey information. Let's take a look at some of these icons:

- The **green lightning** bolt indicates that your **Apple Watch** is charging.
- The **red lightning** bolt indicates that your **Apple Watch** battery is low and needs to be charged.
- The **lock** indicates that your **Apple Watch** is locked.
- The **airplane** shows that Airplane mode is currently on.
- The **crescent moon** indicates that Do Not Disturb mode is currently on.
- The **masks** indicate that Theater Mode is on.
- The **Wi-Fi** icon indicates that your **Apple Watch** is connected to a nearby Wi-Fi network.
- The **cellular data** icon indicates that your **Apple Watch** is connected to a cellular network.
- The **slashed phone** icon shows that your **Apple Watch** is not connected to your iPhone.
- The **water drop** indicates that your **Apple Watch** is in Water Lock mode.
- The **red dot** indicates that you have notifications to view.
- The **arrow** indicates that an app is using your location services.
- The **bed** indicates that your **Apple Watch** is in Sleep mode.

Brightness & Text Size

- Open the **Settings menu** and tap on **Display & Brightness.**
- Here you will find options to make the **display brighter or dimmer.** Drag the slider across the screen or use the **Digital Crown** to adjust these settings.
- You will also find the option to **change the text size** and **make it bold** to suit your needs. Drag the slider to make the font bigger, or turn the **Digital Crown**.

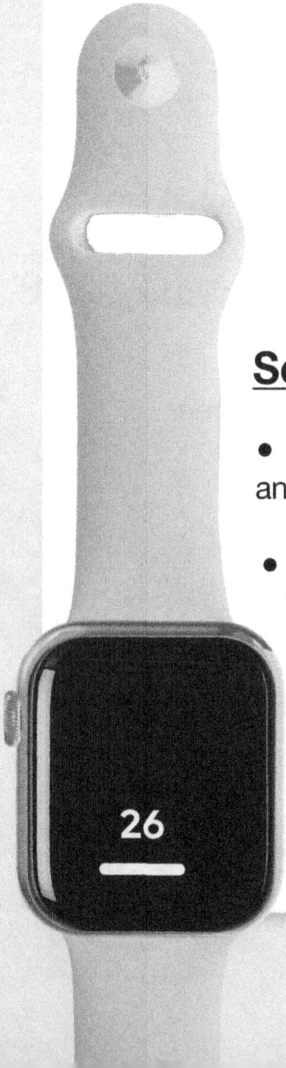

Sounds & Haptics

- To change the alert volume on your **Apple Watch**, open the **Settings app** and select Sound & Haptics.
- Here you can adjust the volume by dragging the slider or by turning the **Digital Crown**.
- You can also choose to put your **Apple Watch** into silent mode. Haptics include all the vibrational alerts on your **Apple Watch**.

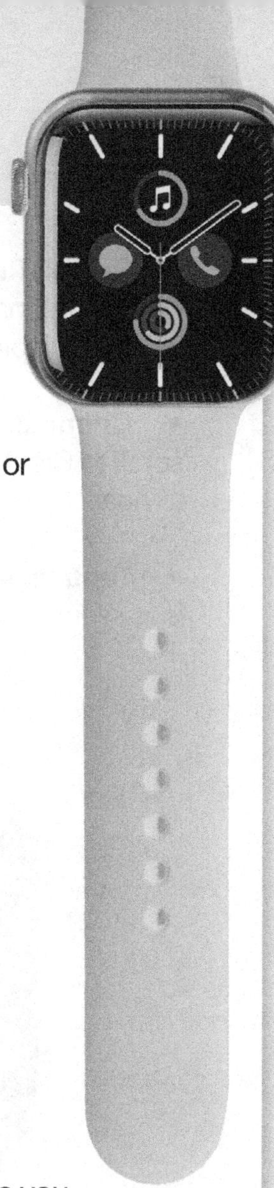

- Adjust the intensity of the Haptics by opening the **Settings app** and selecting Sounds & Haptics.
- You will see the option to turn **Haptic alerts on or off.**
- You can choose different intensity levels, such as the default settings or more prominent settings.

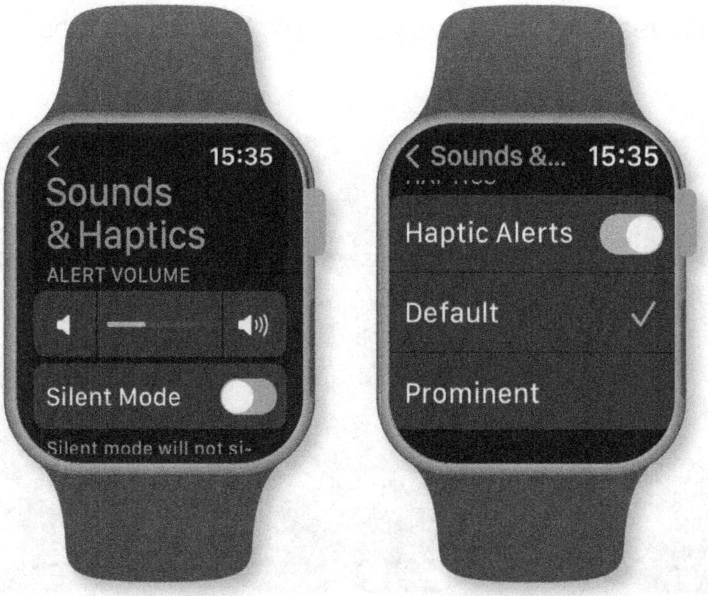

Your **Apple Watch** also has haptic responses in the **Digital Crown**. This allows you to feel clicks when you turn the crown to scroll through different menus, giving your **Apple Watch** the feeling of being a real mechanical watch. You can turn Haptics on or off.

- Open the **Settings** and go to **Sounds & Haptics.**
- Toggle the option for **Crown Haptics** to turn this feature on or off.

Speak Time

Your **Apple Watch** can tell you the time in many different ways, and there are a few features specifically designed to aid those with visual impairments.

- **Raising your wrist** is the most basic gesture you can use to view the time. When you raise your wrist, you will see the time appear on your watch face.

- **Speak Time:** this feature allows you to hear the time spoken out loud by your **Apple Watch**. To enable this feature, go to the **Settings app** and scroll down to Clock. When you hold the display with two fingers, your Apple Watch will read the time aloud.

- **Chimes:** set your **Apple Watch** to chime at the start of every hour. In the **Settings app**, scroll to Clock and turn on Chimes. You can also choose what type of sound you would like to hear.

- **Taptics:** this is a great feature that allows your **Apple Watch** to tap out the time when it is in silent mode.

◊ To turn on **Taptic Time**, open the **Settings app** and scroll to Clock.

◊ Select Taptic Time and toggle the switch to turn it on.

◊ You will have three different options to choose from:

◊ **Digits:** you will feel long taps for every 10 hours and short taps for every subsequent hour, followed by long taps for each 10-minute interval and short taps for every following minute.

◊ For example, if the time is 16:58, you will feel one long tap followed by six short taps, then five long taps followed by eight short taps.

◊ **Terse:** you will feel a long tap for every 5-hour interval and short taps for the subsequent hours, followed by a long tap for each quarter-hour.

◊ **Morse Code:** each digit of the time will be tapped out in morse code using long and short taps.

- **Siri:** you can always use Siri to carry out many different tasks, including telling the time. Just raise your wrist and say, "What time is it?" and Siri will respond to your request.

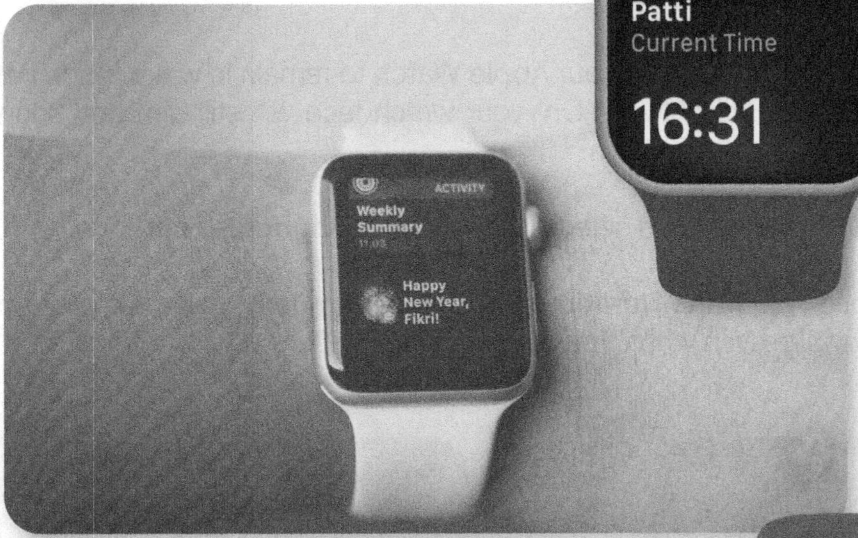

Enable Always-On

The Always-On feature allows your Apple Watch display to stay on. When your wrist is down, the display will still dim, and only the data that you have selected will be shown. When you raise your wrist, the **Apple Watch** will awake fully.

- Open the **Settings app** and scroll to **Display & Brightness.**

- Scroll to the bottom of this menu to find the **Always-On option.**

- Turn **Always-On** on; then you can configure some additional settings:

Show Complication Data: This option allows you to choose which complications (special features) you want to see when your wrist is down.

- **Show Notifications:** This option allows you to select which notifications you want to see when your wrist is down.

- **Show Apps:** This option allows you to select which apps you want to be visible when your wrist is down.

Sleep mode

You can change how long you want your **Apple Watch** to remain in wake mode before it goes to sleep. Even when you use Always-On, your watch face will still dim and show only your selected data when your wrist is down.

- Open the **Settings app** and select the **Display & Brightness settings.**

- Find the option for **Wake Duration** and choose how long you want your **Apple Watch** to stay awake even when you are not using it.

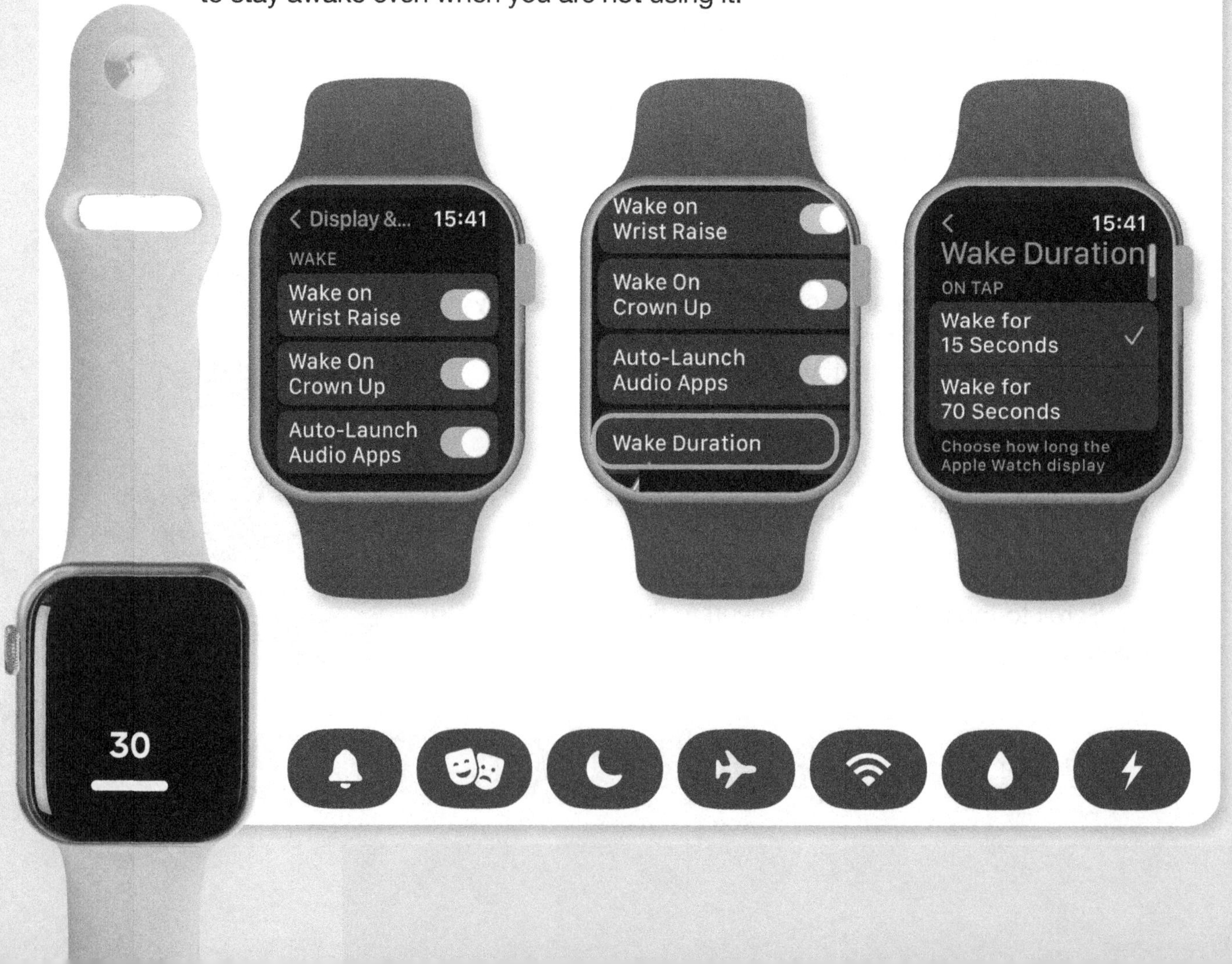

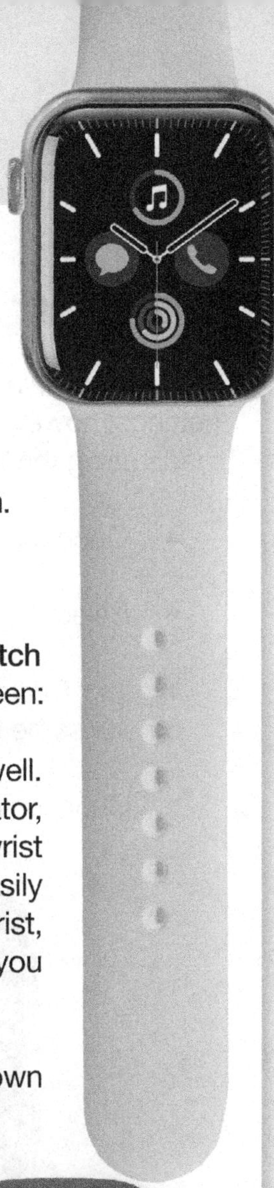

Returning to the Clock Face

You can configure how long you want your apps to remain open before the **Apple Watch** returns to your default watch face.

- To change these settings, open the **Settings app** on the **Apple Watch**.
- In the General settings, find the option for Return to Clock.

- Scroll down and select how long your **Apple Watch** should wait before returning to the watch face screen: Always, After 2 minutes, After 1 hour, etc.

You can select custom times for each app as well. This is a useful feature for apps like the Calculator, where you may be busy with a task and your wrist will often be facing down. However, you can easily return to the calculator simply by raising your wrist, and the app will remain open for however long you choose.

- In the Return to Clock settings, scroll down to find a list of installed apps.
- Tap on the app and select a custom time.

Returning to App

You may wish to set your **Apple Watch** so that it returns to the app you last opened when it went to sleep. This is useful for apps like Music or Stopwatch. You may be listening to music on your **Apple Watch** for a long time so that the display goes to sleep. However, upon raising your wrist, it will return you directly to the music app.

- In the **Settings app**, scroll to **General settings** and then select **Return to Clock**.
- Scroll down to the app you want to set, and tap on it.
- **Turn on** the setting for **"Return to App"**.

Language

Your **Apple Watch** language settings will automatically sync with your **iPhone** language settings; however, you can choose a different language. Howeve , these changes can only be made using the Watch app on your **iPhone.**

- Open the **Watch App** and go to **General Settings.**
- Select **Language & Region.**
- Tap Custom (you must select Custom because you are changing settings that would otherwise be the same across all your Apple devices) and then select Watch Language.
- Choose which language you would like to set your **Apple Watch** to.

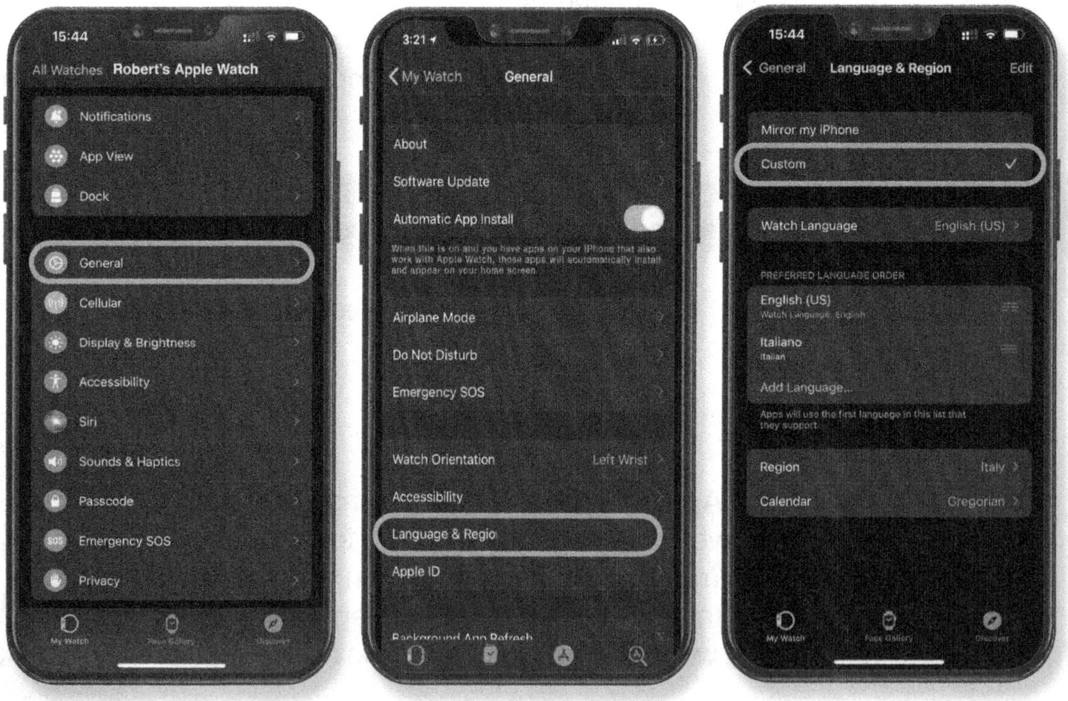

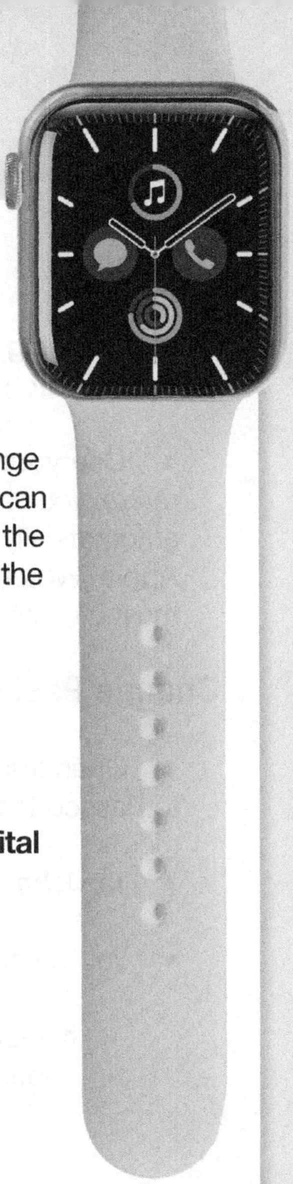

Orientation

When you set up your **Apple Watch** for the first time, it will ask you which wrist you will wear it on, which determines the device's orientation settings. If you choose to wear the device on your other wrist, you will need to change the orientation settings, or the display will be upside down. Similarly, you can wear the **Apple Watch** with the **Digital Crown** facing the left side instead of the right side, which is the default. This change will also require you to change the orientation settings.

- Open the **Settings app** on your **Apple Watch.**
- Go to **General settings** and **select Orientation.**
- You will be able to select your right or left wrist and choose if the **Digital Crown** faces the left or right.

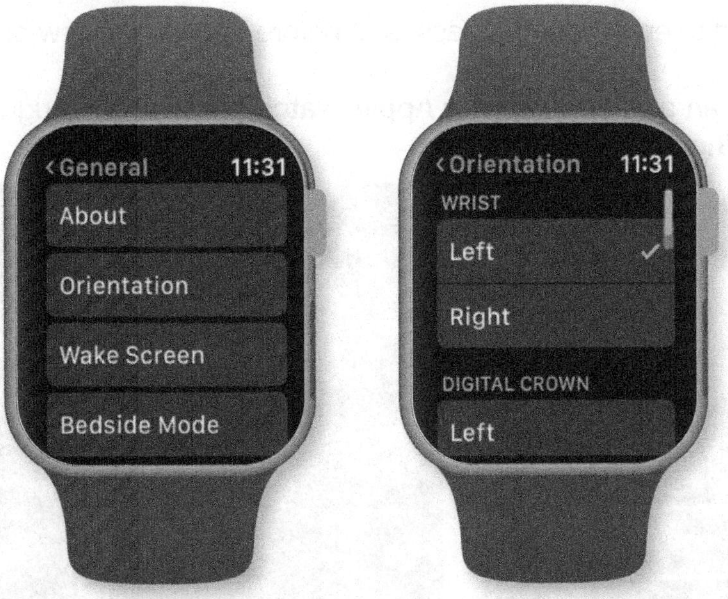

Passcodes

You will need to set a passcode on your **Apple Watch** if you have the Apple Pay feature set up, but it is also essential for protecting all of the data stored on your watch. You will be asked to set a passcode the first time you set up your **Apple Watch**, but you can turn this feature off or change the passcode.

Unlocking

- **Entering your passcode:** raise your wrist to wake up your **Apple Watch** and input your 4-digit code onto the number pad.

- **Use your iPhone:** if you have your **iPhone** within close range, you can simply unlock it to unlock your **Apple Watch** automatically. This feature will only work if your **iPhone** and **Apple Watch** can communicate via Bluetooth, and they must be within range of each other.

Change Passcode

- Open the **Settings app** on your **Apple Watch** and scroll down to Passcode to change your passcode.

- Tap **Change Passcode.**

- You will need to enter your old passcode before choosing a new one.

  - You can also change your **Apple Watch** passcode through the **Watch app** on your **iPhone.**

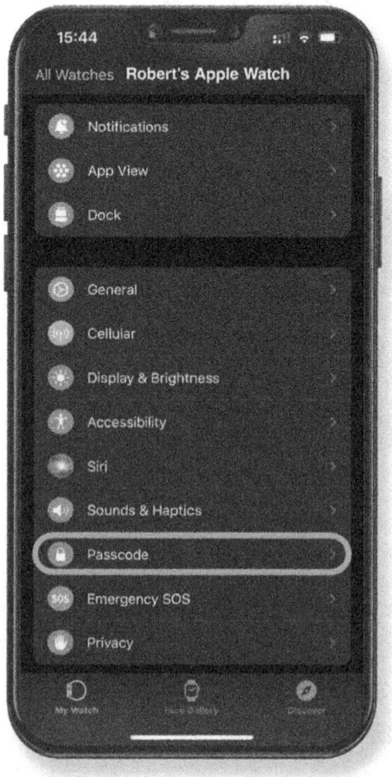

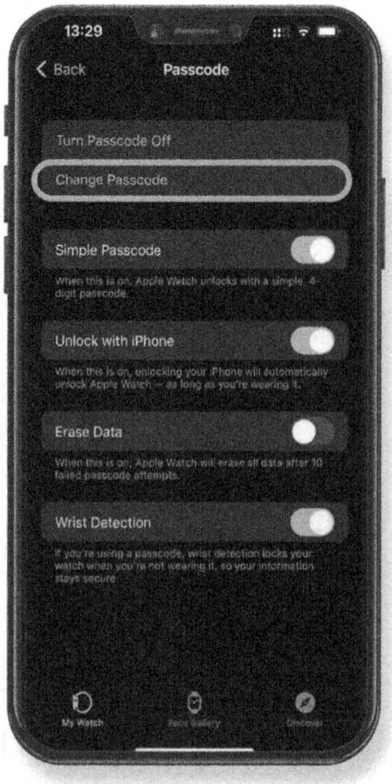

Turn off Passcode

- Open the **Settings app** on your **Apple Watch** and scroll down to Passcode to turn off your passcode.
- Tap the option to **Turn Passcode Off.**
- You will be asked to enter your passcode before turning it off.
- Keep in mind that features such as Apple Pay will be disabled if your passcode is turned off.

Automatic Lock

Your **Apple Watch** will automatically lock itself when you are not wearing it, and you will have to enter your passcode when you put it back on your wrist. You can turn this feature off, but this will limit most of the smart features on your **Apple Watch**.

- Open the **Settings app** on your **Apple Watch** and scroll down to Passcode.
- Tap **Wrist Detection** and select whether you want this feature turned on or off.

Manual Lock

- To lock your **Apple Watch**, open the **Control Center** by touching and holding the bottom of the screen and then swiping up.
- Tap the lock icon.

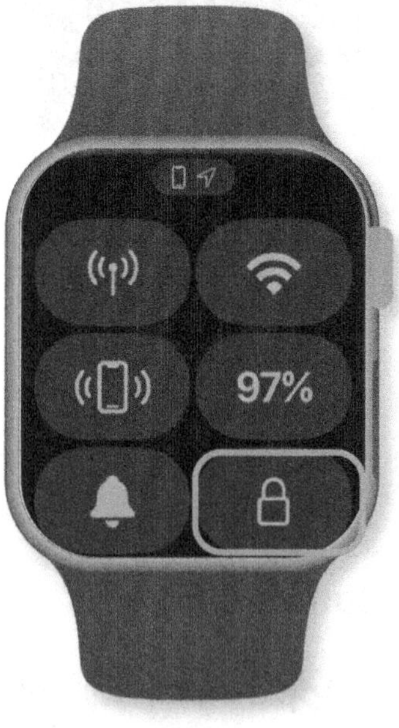

Forgot Your Passcode

You cannot retrieve a lost **Apple Watch** passcode, and you should try to make sure you never forget it. If you cannot remember your passcode, you will have to erase all of the data on your **Apple Watch** and reset it.

- First, unpair your **Apple Watch** from your **iPhone** by opening the **Watch app.**

- Find your watch under the **All Watches tab**. Tap the **Info icon** on the right side, then **select Unpair.** You will need to confirm your choice.
- You may also be asked to enter your Apple ID password.
- Your **iPhone** will create a backup of your **Apple Watch** before unpairing.
- Next, you must reset your **Apple Watch**:
  - ◊ Place the watch on its charger.
  - ◊ **Press and hold the side button** until you see the **Power Off option.**
  - ◊ Now press and hold the **Digital Crown** until you see the reset option.
  - ◊ Tap Reset.
- Your **Apple Watch** will not reset itself, which can take a few minutes.
- When it is done, you can pair it with your **iPhone** by following the same steps from Chapter 2. Select "Restore From Backup" and not "Set Up as New **Apple Watch**".

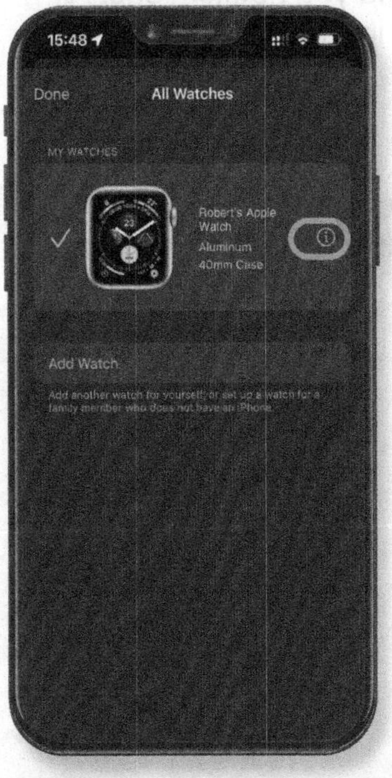

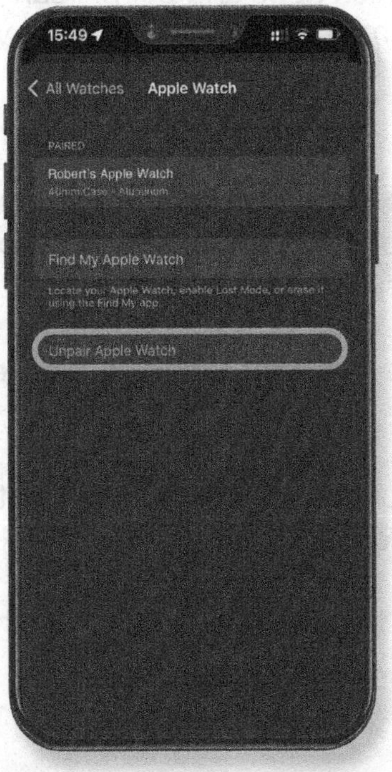

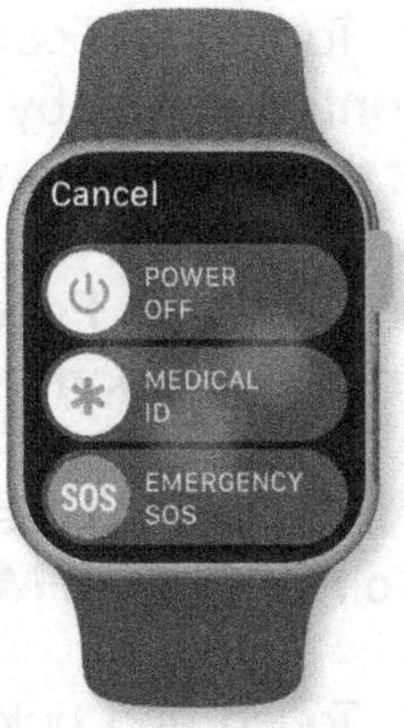

Unlock Attempts

You can protect the information on your **Apple Watch** by turning on a setting that will erase all of your data when an incorrect passcode is entered for 10 consecutive attempts.

- Open the **Settings app** and go to the **Passcode menu.**
- **Turn on Erase Data** to enable this feature.
- This does not stop you from unlocking your **Apple Watch** with your **iPhone.**

Focus

Focus is a feature you can use on your **iPhone** and **Apple Watch** devices. **It is designed to help you stay focused by reducing distractions.** You can create a Focus schedule to suit many activities, and when it is turned on, you will only receive notification that you have selected.

For example, you can create a Focus schedule for Sleep by choosing a start and end time and selecting which apps and people can send you notifications. All other distractions will be muted until the Focus is over in the morning.

Turn on Focus

- To turn on Focus on your **Apple Watch**, open the **control center** by touching and holding the bottom of the screen, then swiping up.
- Find the **Focus button**, shaped like a **crescent moon.**
- You can tap this button to turn on the default **Do Not Disturb Mode**.
- Touch and hold this button to open up the **Focus menu.**

Here you will find some preinstalled Focus schedules, including Do Not Disturb

Here you will find some preinstalled Focus schedules, including **Do Not Disturb, Driving, Personal, Sleep, and Work.**

- Tap on the Focus schedule you would like to turn on and select how long you want to focus. Choose between On, On for 1 hour, On until tomorrow morning, or On until I leave, etc.
- Once you have chosen a Focus schedule other than Do Not Disturb, it will show up in the Control Center, where you can tap it without entering the menu.
- When activated, the Focus icon will appear at the top of your device display.
- Turn off Focus by tapping the icon in the Control center.

Create a Custom Focus Schedule

You can create your own custom Focus schedule using your **iPhone.**

- **Open the Settings app on your iPhone** and scroll to Focus.
- In the Focus menu, you can find some existing Focus schedules just like on your Apple Watch—**Do Not Disturb, Sleep, Personal, and Work.**

- You can tap any of these schedules to access further personalization settings:

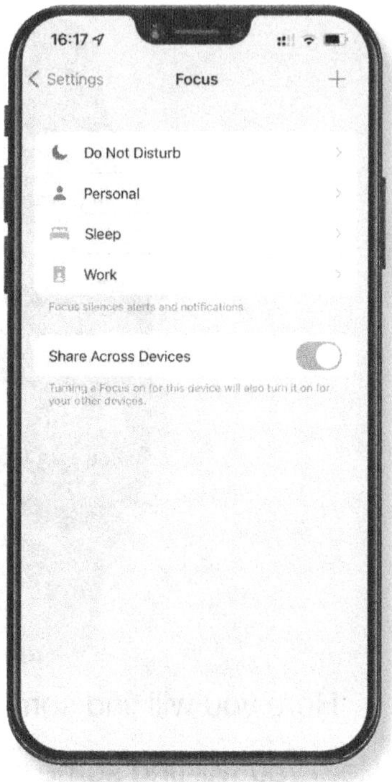

- Allowed notifications from specifiied people and apps.

- Choose whether to notify your contacts that you have notifications silenced.

- Choose to hide notification badges from your Home Screen.

- Choose to show silenced notifications on your Lock Screen.

- Set start and end times.

- At the top left of the screen, you will see a **[+]** sign. Tapping this icon will allow you to create **custom Focus schedules.**

- In the Focus menu, you will also see the **option to Share Across Devices**. Turning this on will allow you to sync your Focus schedules with your **Apple Watch** and all other devices on your Apple ID.

Power

Check Battery Status

Monitor the power on your **Apple Watch** to make sure you are never stuck in a situation where it has run out of battery.

- To check how much power remains in the battery, open the control center by touching and holding the bottom of the screen and then swiping upwards.

- You will see an icon with a battery status indicator **(%)**.

- Tapping this icon will open the battery menu where you can turn on Power Reserve mode. If you have Bluetooth devices such as headphones connected, you can also see their remaining battery life here.

- You can also add a complication to your watch face (see next section to learn more about complications and watch faces) that shows you your remaining battery life.

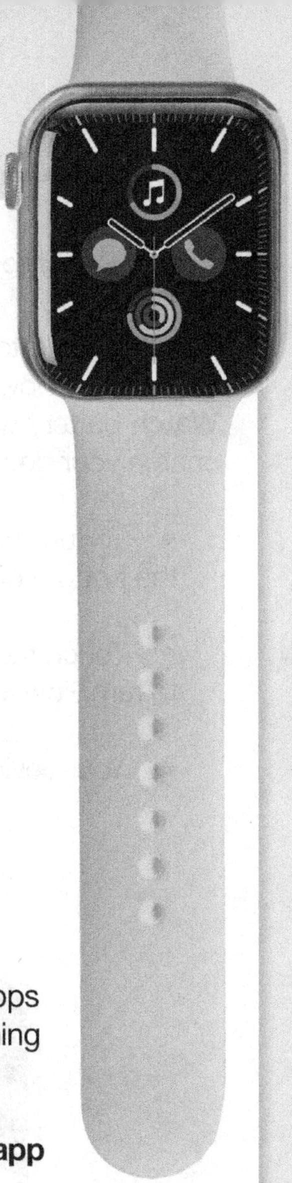

Prevent Background App Refresh

You can reduce power consumption on your **Apple Watch** by preventing apps from refreshing in the background. This prevents apps from updating or searching for new content while not in use.

- Open the **Settings app** and select **General.**
- Tap Background **App Refresh**, and turn this feature off.
- You can also turn this off for specific apps and not for others.
- Apps that are installed and have complications on your watch face will continue to refresh even if Background App Refresh is turned off.

Power Reserve Mode

Your **Apple Watch** will automatically alert you when your battery level reaches 10% and remind you to enter Power Reserve mode. This feature is designed to help extend the life of your **Apple Watch** battery when it is low. It can give you a few extra hours of run time when you cannot charge your device, allowing you to see the time but preventing apps from running.

- To turn **Power Reserve mode on**, open the **Control Center** by touching and holding the bottom of the display and then swiping upwards.
- Touch the battery icon **(%)**, and a new menu will appear where you can drag the slider to turn Power Reserve on.
- Your device will return to a normal power mode when you charge it.

Accessibility

There are several features installed on your **Apple Watch** that help to make it more accessible to people with any kind of impairment.

VoiceOver

This feature is useful for people with vision impairments or those using their watches in situations where they may not be able to see the screen.

VoiceOver allows you to interact with the display differently, and your watch will read out each item or menu you select.

- The best way to activate VoiceOver is to use Siri, since you will likely be unable to see the display. Simply raise your wrist and say, "Turn VoiceOver on."

- You can also turn VoiceOver on by opening the **Settings app** on your **Apple Watch** and scrolling to **Accessibility**. Open this menu and select **VoiceOver to turn it on.**

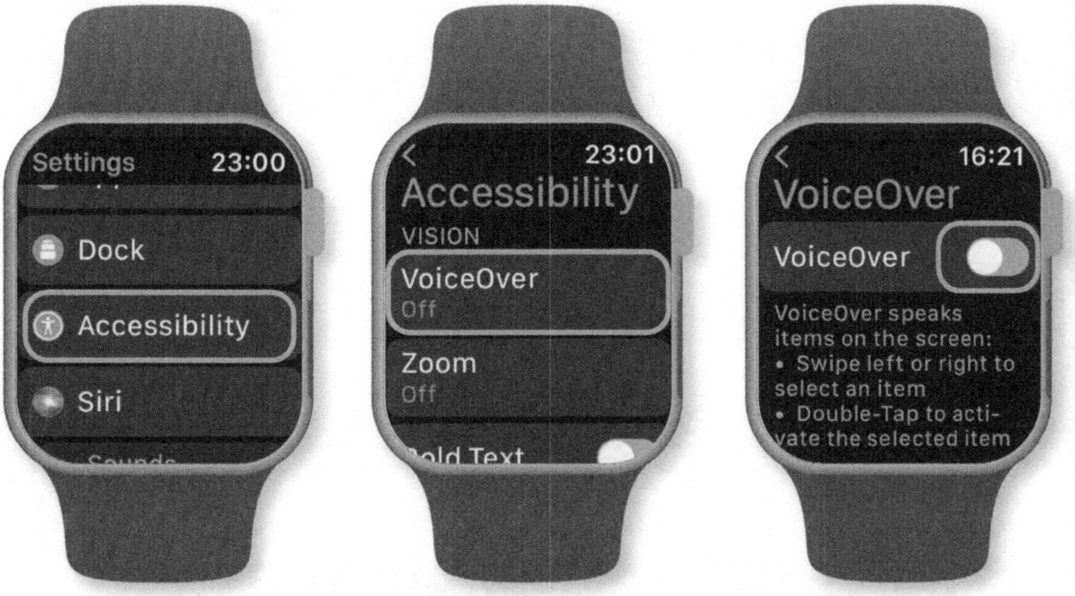

- Use these gestures to control your **Apple Watch** with VoiceOver:

  ◊ Explore your display by moving your finger over the screen. VoiceOver will read out each item that you touch. Simply swipe up, down, left, or right to view other pages.

  ◊ Go back by tracing a 'Z' shape with two fingers on the display.

  ◊ Select an item by double-tapping. This will act upon the last item that VoiceOver spoke of.

Assistive Touch

This is another accessiblity feature designed to aid people who have difficulties touching the screen or pressing buttons, such as those with neurological disabilities, severe arthritis, or amputees. You can use your **Apple Watch** hands-free. It allows you to use various gestures to carry out actions on your **Apple Watch** instead of tapping icons on the screen or pressing buttons.

- Activate **AssistiveTouch** by opening the **Settings app** on your **Apple Watch**.
- Scroll to Accessibility and select AssistiveTouch, where you can turn the feature on.
- Tap **Hand Gestures** and select On.

Click the Learn More button to see interactive animations that can help you become accustomed to the gestures.

- With **AssistiveTouch,** you can perform the following actions:
  - ◊ **Clench** your fist to tap.
  - ◊ **Pinch** to go forward.
  - ◊ **Double pinch** to go back.
  - ◊ **Double clench** to visit the Assistive Touch Action menu.

To activate the **stopwatch** using AssistiveTouch, for example, you can do the following:

- Activate Assistive Touch by double clenching.
- Pinch to move the selection forward until you land on the Press Crown action.
- Select this action by clenching.
- Scroll through the apps on the Home Screen by pinching to go forward and double pinching to go back.
- When you land on the stopwatch app, select it by clenching.

Zoom

If you are struggling to see the text and icons on the small display of your **Apple Watch**, try using the zoom feature. This will magnify the contents on the display, making them easier to read.

- To turn on Zoom, open the **Settings app** on your **Apple Watch**.
- Scroll to **Accessibility** settings, and then select **Zoom.**
- You can also access these settings through the Watch app on your **iPhone**:
    - ◊ Select **My Watch**
    - ◊ Tap **Accessibility**
    - ◊ Select **Zoom**

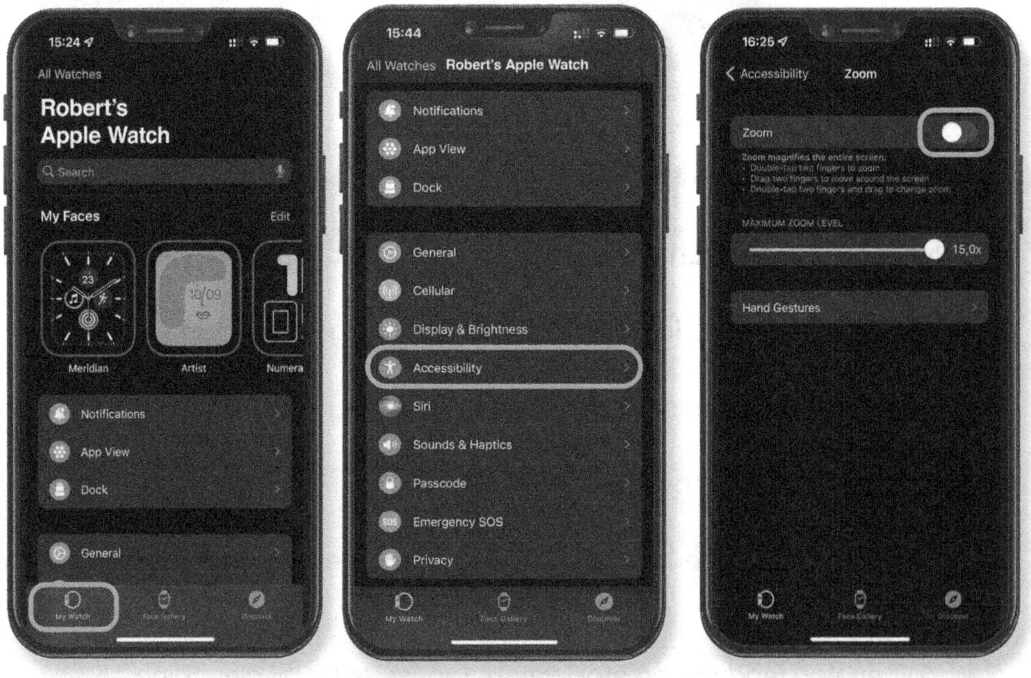

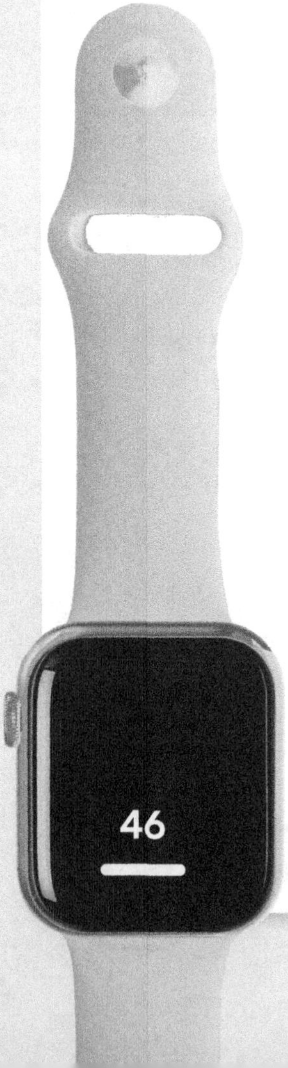

Now you can double-tap your display to zoom in or out whenever you need to.

- Drag two fingers across the screen to pan and move around.
- You can also use the **Digital Crown** to scroll up and down.
- To increase or decrease the magnification level, use two fingers to double-tap and hold the display, then drag it up or down.

Audio Balance

Your **Apple Watch** and **iPhone** will be set to a combined left and right audio balance by default, so when you use earphones, headphones, or AirPods, the sound will come out of both sides equally. However, you can change these settings to favor one side or the other if you have hearing issues.

- To access these settings, open the **Settings app** on your **Apple Watch**.
- Tap **Accessibility** and then **Hearing**.
- You can change the audio from stereo (left and right balance) to mono (favors left or right).
- If you choose to use mono audio, you can use the slider to adjust which side you need the sounds to come from.

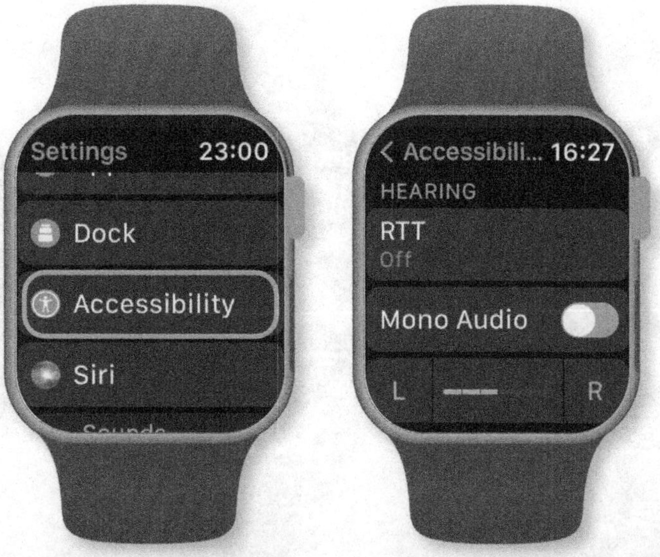

Siri

No Apple device would be complete without Siri, the voice-controlled virtual assistant. Siri is integrated into your **Apple Watch** and you can use it just like you do on your **iPhone**.

The small display size on an **Apple Watch can make it difficult** to carry out some tasks, but Siri can easily carry these out for you.

To activate Siri on your **Apple Watch**, all you need to do is:

- **Say "Hey Siri"**
- Or, press down and hold the **Digital Crown**.
- You will see the Siri icon appear and wait for you to make a request.

If this doesn't work, you can check to see if Siri is turned on for your **Apple Watch**:

- Press the **Digital Crown** to see your apps on the Home Screen.
- Select the **Settings app**.
- Scroll to **Siri** and press it.

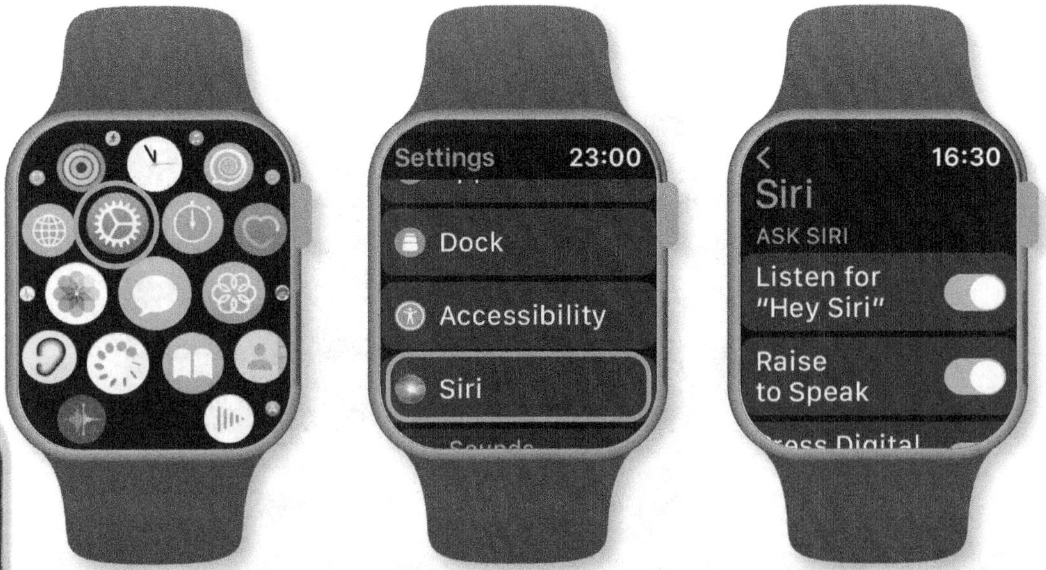

- Make sure that all the options—**Hey Siri**, **Raise to Speak**, and **Press Digital Crown**—are toggled to the **on position.**

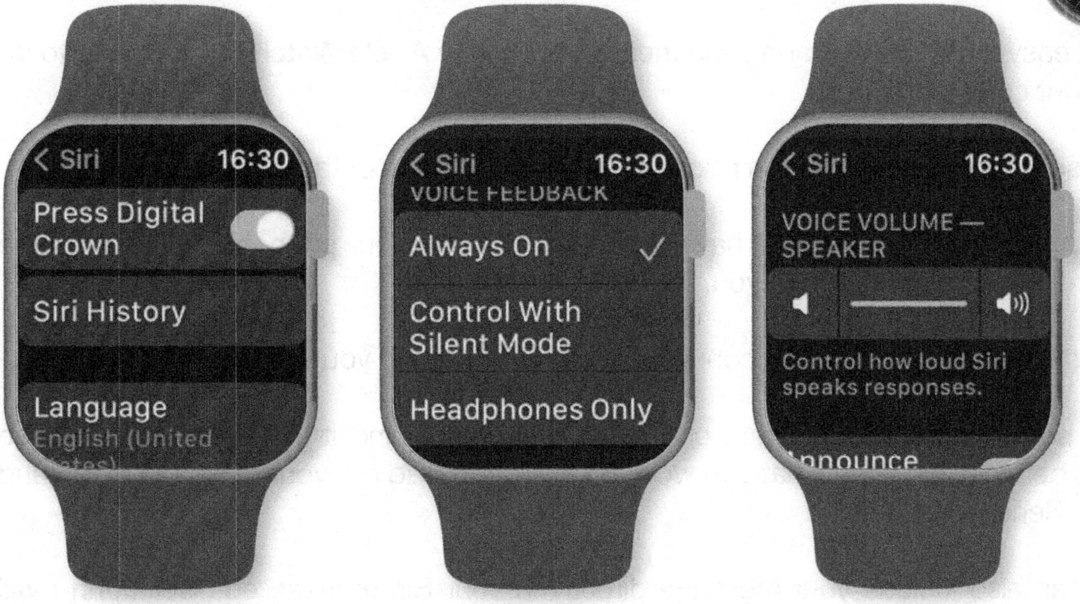

You can use Siri to make basic requests:

- "What is the time?"
- "What is the weather going to be today?"
- "Open the Photos app".
- "Start a 10-minute timer".
- "Tell my wife I will be home at 7 pm".
- "What is my heart rate?"
- "What song is playing?"
- "Convert inches into millimeters".
- "Start tracking my exercise."
- "Do a rap" or "Sing a song".

You can also ask Siri how it can help you further.

Messaging

Siri makes it easy to write, reply, and send messages on your **Apple Watch**. All you need to do is give the right command:

- **Call someone:** Siri can start a phone call with any of the contacts in your phonebook.

- **Call a number:** If you do not have a contact saved in your phonebook, just read the number to Siri, who will dial it for you.

- **Redial my last call:** Instantly connect with the last person you spoke to.

- **Text someone:** Tell Siri to text one of your contacts, and it will open the message dialogue, before asking you what you would like to say. Read out your message to Siri and then say "Send."

- You can also include your message directly in your Siri request, eg, "Tell John I will meet him at the corner." Siri will compose a message to John saying "I will meet you at the corner."

- You can also ask Siri to read out your last message or the last message from a specific contact.

Calendars and Timekeeping

Siri is seamlessly integrated into your **Apple Watch**'s clock, schedule, and calendar functions. Ask Siri to do anything from setting an alarm to calculating how long until your next doctor's appointment:

- "What is the time?"
- "What is the next appointment on my calendar?"
- "What is the time in Minnesota?"
- "What time is sunrise tomorrow?"
- "When is Sue's birthday?"

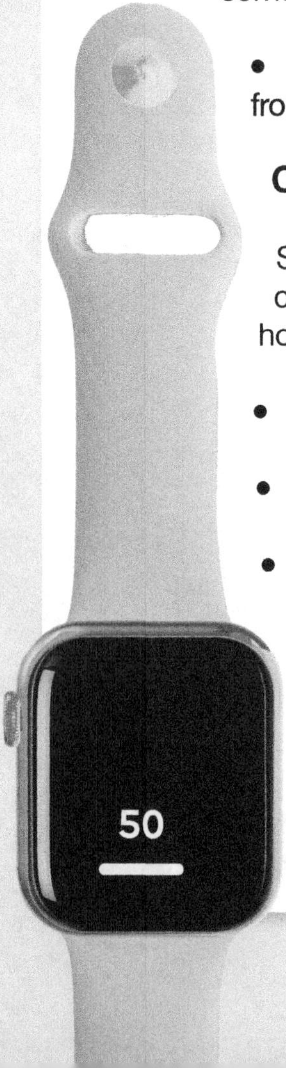

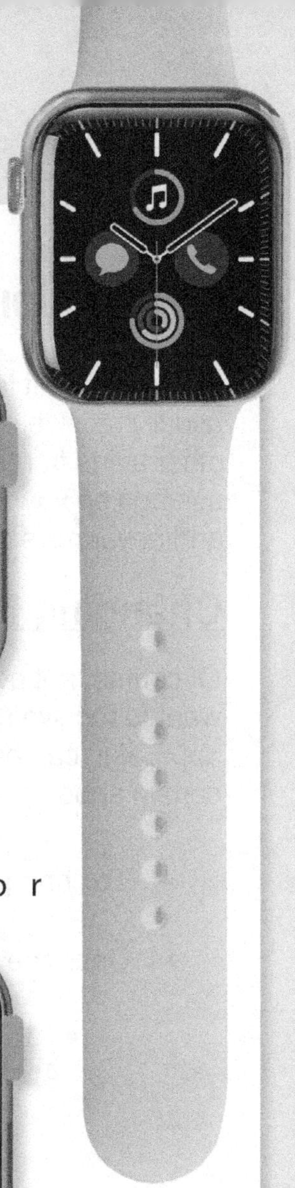

- "When is my next appointment with Dr. Schafer?"
- "Set an alarm for 6:30 tomorrow morning."
- "Start a stopwatch."
- "Create an event for August 5th at noon."
- "Make a note."
- "Remind me to buy toothpaste next time I visit the store."

Navigation

You can use Siri to navigate using Apple Maps or Google Maps if you have the apps installed on your **iPhone** and synced with your **Apple Watch**. You can ask Siri where a location is, or to give you directions:

- "Where is the nearest grocery store?"
- "Direct me to a gas station."

More From Siri

Siri is not only a useful assistant, it can perform many tasks you may not have thought of.

- **Translation:** Use Siri to translate phrases from one language into another. This makes traveling much easier as you can communicate with people in their own foreign language.
- **Apple Pay:** Use Siri to send money to one of your contacts.
- **Turn settings on or off:** Siri can turn on Do Not Disturb, Airplane, or Focus, as well as most other settings on your **Apple Watch**.
- **Flip a coin:** Use Siri to flip a coin in a game of chance.

Notifications

One of the best features of the **Apple Watch** is the ability to see all of the notifications you would usually receive on your **iPhone**, including your messages, phone calls, emails, invitations, and other alerts from your apps. The notifications on your Apple Watch will be set to mirror the settings on your **iPhone** by default. This makes it much easier to stay in touch with your family and never miss any important communication.

Changing Notification Settings

Of course, not everybody wants notifications and communications on their wrist. Perhaps you want to receive notifications from your fitness and health apps but not from your communication apps. You can easily turn this feature off or choose to see only selected notifications from certain apps or contacts.

- To change your notification settings, you will need to use our **iPhone.**
- Open the **Watch app** on your **iPhone**, then select **Notifications.**
    - You will see some options and then a list of all the compatible apps for your **Apple Watch**.

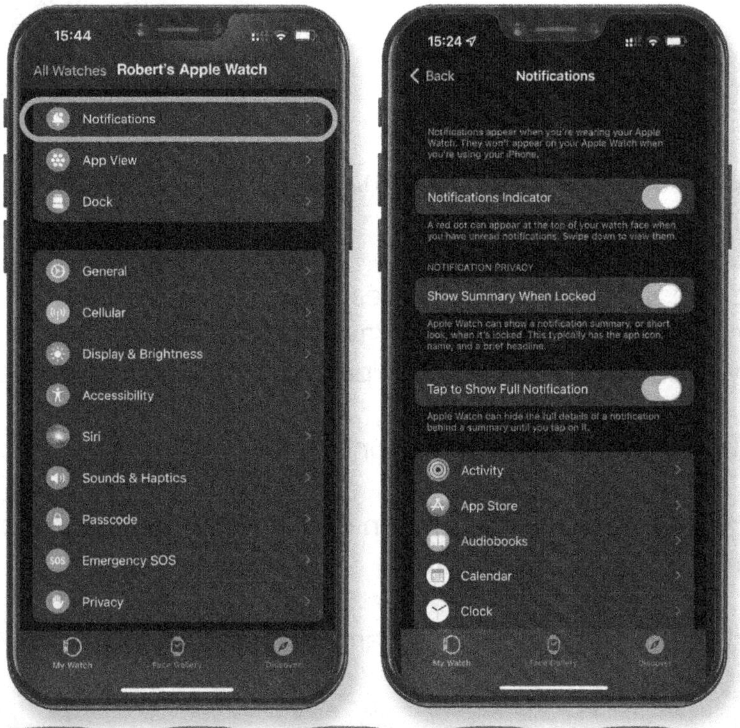

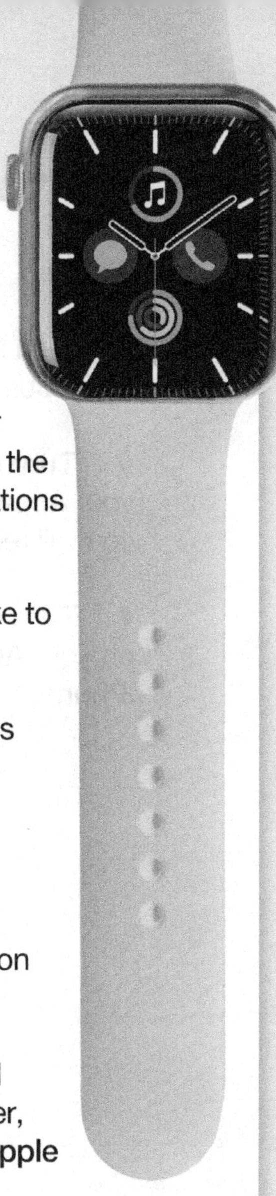

◊ **Notifications Indicator:** Toggle this setting to show or hide a red dot at the top of your **Apple Watch**'s display when you have unread notifications.

◊ **Show Summary When Locked:** Toggle this setting to allow your **Apple Watch** to show a short summary of your notifications, including the app icon and name, and a brief headline of the contents of the notifications when the device is locked.

◊ **Tap to Show Full Notification:** Toggle this setting if you would like to be able to tap a notification summary to open the full details.

◊ **Show Notifications on Wrist Down:** Choose to show notifications on your Apple Watch even when your wrist is down.

- Scroll through the list of apps and choose the notification settings for each of them.

- You will see the option to Mirror My **iPhone** or set Custom notification settings.

- The custom settings offered will be different for each app, but you will generally have the option to Allow Notifications, Send to Notifications enter, or turn Notifications Off. Remember, these changes will only affect your **Apple Watch**, and your iPhone notifications will remain the same as before.

- You can also change the alert settings for the notifications by choosing to turn sounds and Haptics on or off.

Changing Notification Settings on Your Apple Watch

You can access a limited number of notification settings directly on your **Apple Watch**.

- When you receive a notification, swipe left on it and then tap to bring up a small menu where you can choose to:

◊ **Mute for 1 hour:** This action will mute all notifications on your **Apple Watch** for the next hour. You can still see these notifications on your iPhone.

◊ **Mute for Today:** This action will mute all notifications on your **Apple Watch** for the rest of the day. You can still see these notifications on your iPhone.

◊ **Add to Summary:** All future notifications from this particular app will be sent straight to the summary on your **iPhone**.

◊ **Turn off Time Sensitive:** Prevent Time-Sensitive notifications from alerting you on your **Apple Watch**. These notifications ae a special feature associated with Focus, and you will receive them even if you are in a Focus mode.

◊ **Turn off:** This action will stop all notifications from the particular app from appearing on your **Apple Watch**. To turn these notifications back on, visit the Watch app on your **iPhone**.

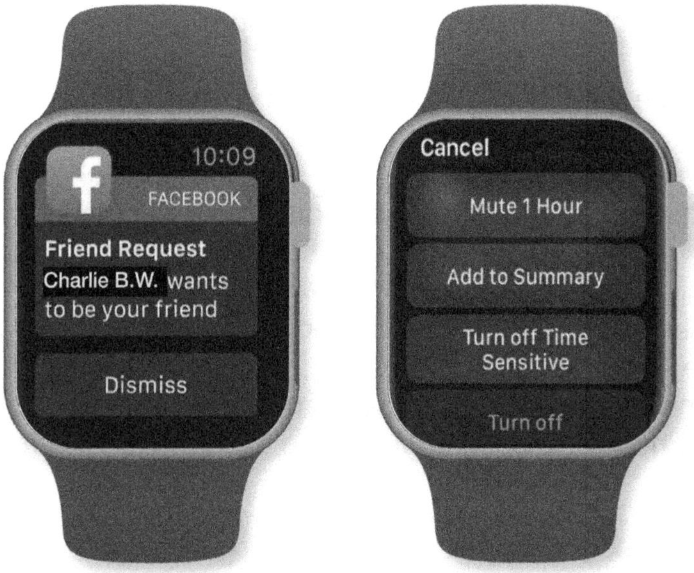

Responding to Notifications

You can respond to notifications using your Apple Watch, or you can save them for a later time if you plan on responding using your **iPhone** instead.

Responding to a Message

When you receive a message notification on your **Apple Watch**, you can read it by raising your wrist and using the **Digital Crown** to scroll down. Dismiss a notification by tapping the Dismiss button at the end of the message or swiping down from the top of the notification. You can also send a reply to the message.

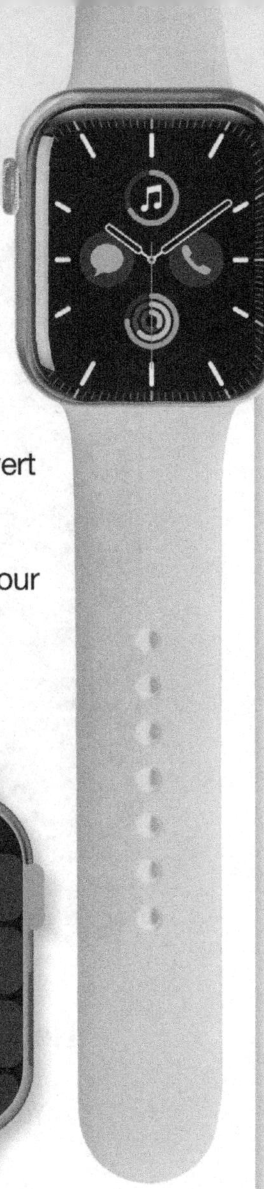

- Using the **Digital Crown**, scroll to the bottom of the message.
- At the bottom, you will see a **Reply button**. Tap it.
- Now you can choose between some of the default message replies; use an emoji, or use Dictate Text, which will use the microphone to convert your spoken words into text.
- You can also choose to compose a reply using the small keyboard on your **Apple Watch**.

You can add your own phrases to the list of default replies that will appear on your **Apple Watch**.

- To do this, use your **iPhone** and go to the **Watch app.**
- Select **My Watch** and then **Messages**.
- Tap **Default Replies,** and then choose **Add Reply**.
- Add your own replies.
- You can rearrange and delete replies here as well.

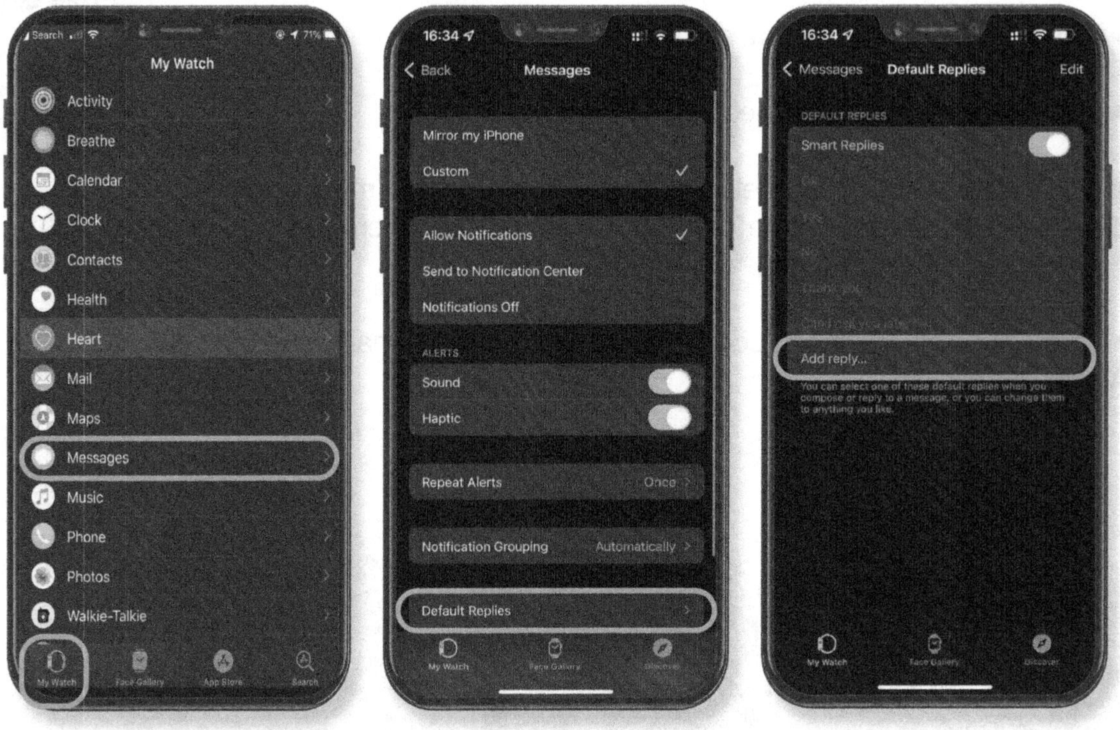

Read and Reply to an Email on Apple Watch

You can easily read and reply to emails on your **Apple Watch** as well.

- To read an email, raise your wrist when you hear or feel the alert.
- You can dismiss the notification by tappin the Dismiss button at the bottom of the notification or by swiping down.
- To reply, hit the Reply button.
- You can choose to reply by:
- composing a message where you can use a QWERTY or QuickPath keyboard. Use the **Digital Crown** to move your cursor within the text.
- using Scribble, where you can use your finger to write out a message that will be converted into text. Use the **Digital Crown** to move the cursor in the text.
- dictating the text so that your **Apple Watch** can convert your spoken

words into text

- using Emojis from the available selection

Watch Faces

Your **Apple Watch** comes with many different watch faces to choose from, and you can download even more using the **Apple Watch** app on your **iPhone**. There are simple and refined watch faces with analog hands and detailed digital faces that can display many data types. The various data fields you can display on your watch face are called 'complications.' You can find many complications preinstalled, but you can also get more by downloading apps on your **iPhone**.

- **A simple analog-style** watch face with no complications.
- **A simple Nike-branded analog-digital** watch face with no complications.
- **The 'infograph'** watch face with analog-style clock hands and numerous complications, including a calendar, day planner, timer, heart rate display, activity tracker, etc.

A good watch face can make a big difference in how you go about your day with the **Apple Watch.** It is essential to find a watch face that you like because you will see a lot of it! Your watch face will serve as the Home Screen on your **Apple Watch**. Make sure you go through all of these options so that your **Apple Watch** can fill its true potential.

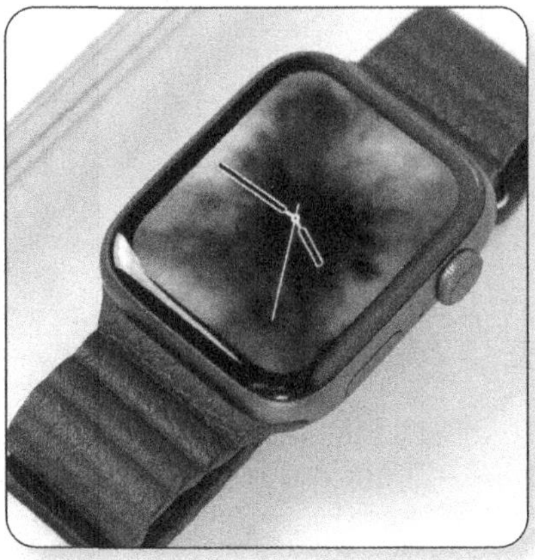

Analog - style

Nike analog - digital

Infograph - style

Switch Watch Faces

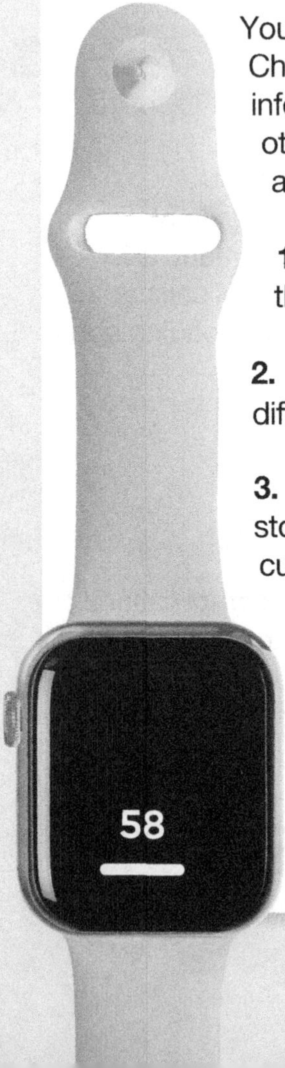

You can easily switch between different watch faces depending on your needs. Choose an informative watch face for your morning where you can see weather information and upcoming events; switch to a watch face with heart rate data and other physical activity stats as you go about your day; and then choose a mindful and calming watch face as you settle down for the evening.

1. Press the **Digital Crown** to show your watch face (this is akin to pressing the home button).

2. Swipe across your digital display from edge to edge to scroll through the different watch faces you have installed.

3. When you land on the one you would like to use, all you need to do is stop swiping. You do not need to press any more buttons. This will become your current watch face.

Some of the watch faces that come standard with your **Apple Watch** include:

- **Activity Analog** shows your activity rings behind an analog-style clock.

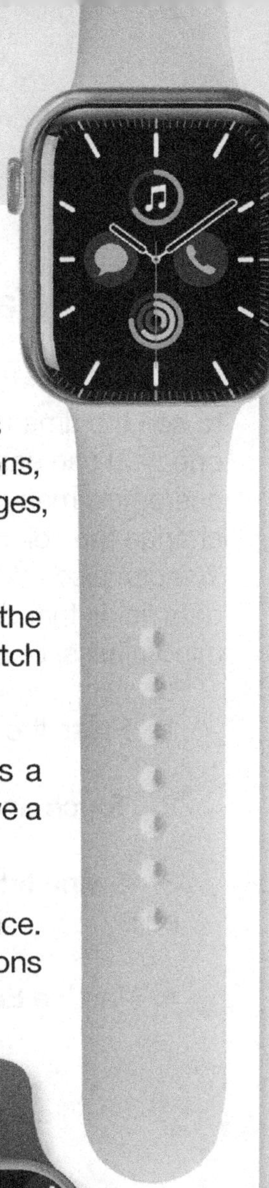

You can add several complications to this watch face, including alarms, audiobooks, blood oxygen, calculator, heart rate, noise, reminders, workouts, etc.

- **Chronograph** has an analog style with more precise time increments and stopwatch features. This face is compatible with several complications, including astronomy, calendar, camera remote, compass, ECG, messages, phone, and world clock.

- **Infograph** has analog-style clock hands and several subdials inside the clock face, and complications on the outer corners. Infograph is a great watch face to display detailed information from your complications.

- **Photos** uses images from your synced album and displays them as a background on your watch face. You can change whether you want to have a digital or analog-style clock, and you can alter the complications.

- **X-large** is a great watch face if you like a simple and clean appearance. It has large, bold text that is easy to read but can display some complications such as blood oxygen, contacts, mail, sleep, etc.

Infograph

Bicolor Digits

Activity Analog

Custom Watch Faces

If you find a watch face you really like to use but prefer to see the time in a digital format rather than an analog one, you can easily customize it. You can also edit and customize many of the available watch faces. You can change the colors or select different data to display. You can also add or remove complications, the various data fields that display information such as weather, mindfulness, or activities.

1. Press the **Digital Crown**.

2. **Touch and hold the display.**

3. **Swipe left or right** to select the watch face you want to edit.

4. Tap the **Edit button.**

5. Depending on which watch face you are editing, you will see different options. Some watch faces allow you to edit many features, while others have limited options.

6. Swipe across the display to select different features to edit. Use the **Digital Crown** to make changes to each of the features.

7. To edit the complications, swipe all the way to the left. You will see each of the complications outlined by a border. Tap on the ones you want to edit, and use the **Digital Crown** to scroll through the available options.

8. To save your edits, simply press the **Digital Crown**.

You can easily create your own watch faces to suit your personal needs.

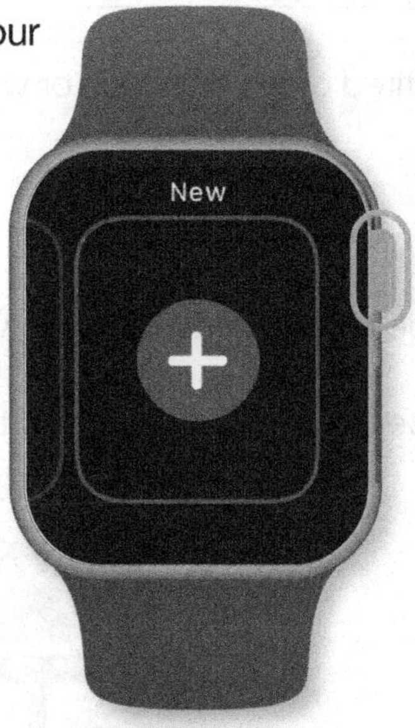

1. Press the **Digital Crown**.

2. Touch and hold the display.

3. Swipe all the way to the right until you see a **[+]** sign. Tap on this button.

4. Use the **Digital Crown** to scroll through all of the available templates.

5. Tap the Add button when you find one you like.

6. If customization options are available, you can scroll through them by swiping across the screen and using the **Digital Crown** to make the edits.

7. When you are done, press the **Digital Crown** to save your new watch face.

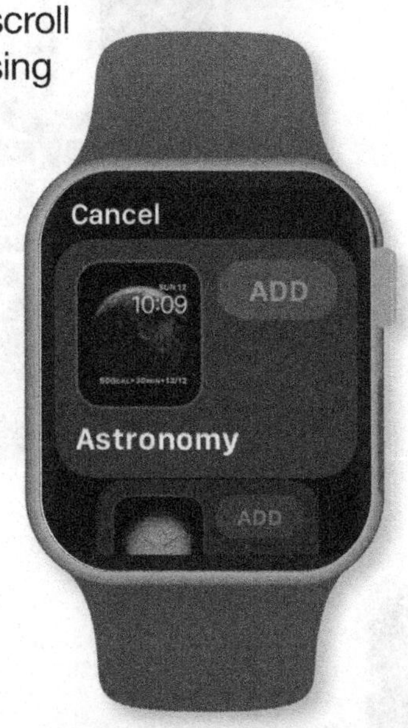

Photos

You can create a custom watch face based on a photo or album of up to 24 photos. This watch face will act as a slideshow, displaying a new photo from the album every time you raise your wrist or tap the display. You can customize the clock face and position, and color fiters, as well as add various complications such as activity, alarms, controls, reminders, shortcuts, stocks, weather, and more. You must have the Photos app installed on your **Apple Watch**, and make sure to sync your desired album.

Deleting Watch Faces

If you grow tired of a watch face or would like to remove it for any reason, you can easily delete it.

1. Press the **Digital Crown**.

2. Swipe to the watch face you want to remove.

3. Swipe up on the display and then **tap the 'Remove' button**.

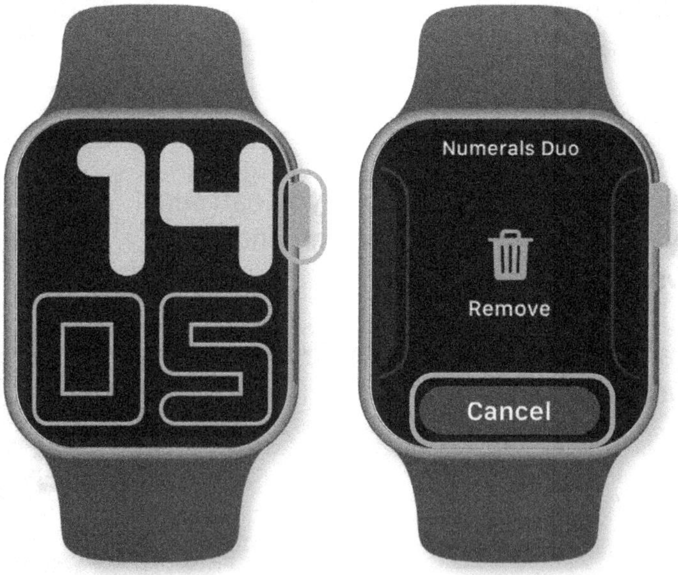

Setting up Apple Pay

Add a Card

You can add a **bank card** through the Watch app on your **iPhone**:

- **Tap My Watch** at the bottom of the screen.
- Select **Wallet & Apple Pay** from the list of apps.
- You can choose to add a card that has been connected to another of your Apple devices by selecting it and entering your card's CVV number.
- If you want to add a new card, tap Add Card, and follow the onscreen instructions to select your banking details, card number, and CVV number.

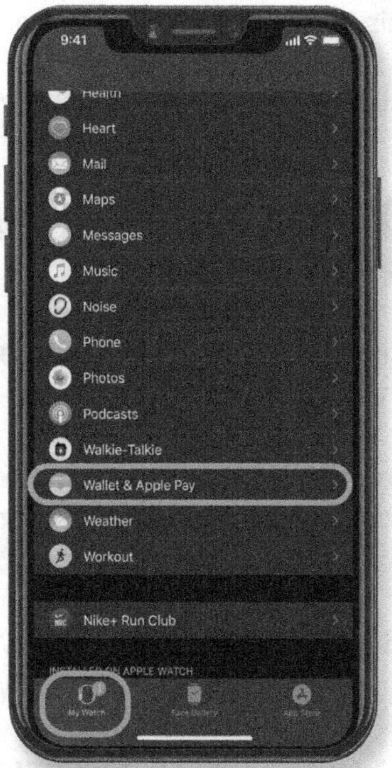

Set your default card on your **Apple Watch** so that your payments will always go through the correct account:

- **Open** the **Watch app** on your **iPhone**.
- **Tap My Watch** at the bottom of the screen.
- **Select Wallet & Apple Pay**
- **Tap Default Card**, and select the one you want to use.

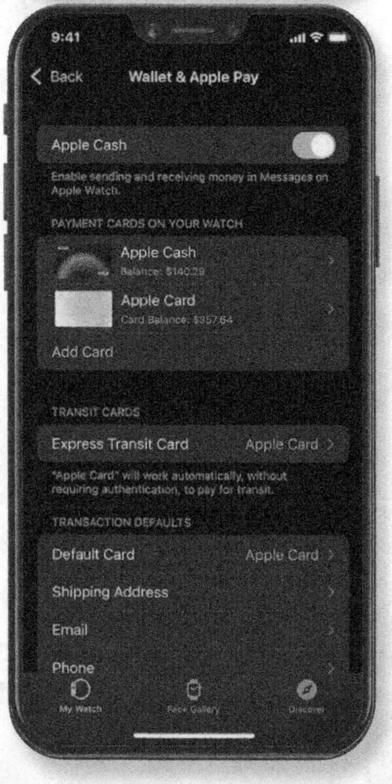

You can easily remove a card from Apple Pay:

- **Open** the **Wallet app** directly on your **Apple Watch.**

- Tap to **select the card** you want to remove.
- Use the **Digital Crown** to scroll down until you see the Remove button.
- Tap this button to remove the card.
- If you want to re-add this card to Apple Pay, you will have to do so through your **iPhone**.

What to Do If Your Apple Watch is Lost or Stolen

You can put your **Apple Watch** into Lost Mode if you ever lose it or have it stolen. This lets you lock and track your missing device. When your **Apple Watch** connects to the internet, you will be notified on your iPhone, and you can then track the device using the Find My app.

Anybody trying to use your watch will need your passcode to access any features, including turning off Find My, erasing your data, or pairing with a new iPhone. They will also need your passcode to access any of your Apple Pay features.

You can send a custom message directly to your **Apple Watch** with your phone number so that if someone does find it and wants to return it, they will be able to contact you.

- Open the **Find My** app on your **iPhone**.
- Tap **Devices** at the bottom of the screen and then **select your Apple Watch.**
- Press **Continue**.
- **Enter your phone number** or a number where someone can reach you and press **Next**.
- You can enter a message to display along with your phone number.
- Press **Activate**.
- **Your Apple Watch will be placed into Lost Mode.**
- You should also receive an email confirming that you have placed your **Apple Watch** into Lost Mode.

If you find your Apple Watch or someone returns it to you, **you can deactivate lost mode by following these steps:**

- Enter your **passcode** on the **Apple Watch**. This will automatically turn Lost Mode off and you can continue to use the device as normal.
- To turn off Lost Mode using your **iPhone**, open the **Find My app** and select your missing **Apple Watch** from the **Devices section.** Select Activated in the Mark As Lost section, and then tap Turn Off Mark As Lost.
- You can also use a computer to turn Lost Mode off by logging in to your icloud.com account with your Apple ID. Select Find **iPhone** and then All Devices. Click on your **Apple Watch** and then Lost Mode. Here you can select Stop Lost Mode.

If you did not have Find My activated on your **Apple Watch** before you lost it or it was stolen, you may not be able to use these functions to find it. In this case, you should take the following steps to protect your information:

- **Change your Apple ID password** by logging in to your **iCloud.com** account.
- **Remove your cards from Apple Pay** on your **iPhone** or **iCloud.com** account.
- Call your bank and let them know which cards may be compromised and alert your local law enforcement that your device was stolen.

CHAPTER 4: Apple Watch Apps

Now that you are familiar with how the **Apple Watch** works, how to navigate, and how to change all your important settings, let's look at some of the apps you can install. Apps make the **Apple Watch** such a great device, allowing you to use it in many different aspects of your life, improving your productivity, helping you stay healthy, and keeping you in touch with the people that matter most.

Viewing and Organizing Your Apps

To see all of the apps installed on your **Apple Watch**, you will need to open the Home Screen by pressing the **Digital Crown**. You will find many different icons arranged in a grid on the Home Screen. Each icon is a shortcut that you can tap to open the app. Unfortunately, if you have many apps installed, you may not be able to see them all, so you can zoom out by turning the **Digital Crown**.

You can touch and hold any app icon to bring up the Edit Apps option. This will let you drag and drop the app into any location on the grid. You can arrange your apps to make them easier to find. A good way to organize your apps is to place your most commonly used icons in and around the center of the grid. You can also arrange your apps into different categories, placing your messaging and mail apps in one corner, photo and audio apps in another, and fitness or productivity apps in another corner. When you are done organizing the apps, simply press the **Digital Crown** to save your changes.

You can organize your apps using the Watch app on your **iPhone** if you have difficulty with the small display on your **Apple Watch**. You need to open the app, select My Watch, and then find the App Layout option from the menu. Here you will see a grid, like the one on your **Apple Watch**. You can easily drag and arrange the apps to suit your needs here.

In the grid view, you will not be able to see the names of the apps, and if you are unfamiliar with what the app icon looks like, it may be challenging to find the right shortcut. However, you can switch from the grid view to a list view instead. All you need to do is press and hold anywhere on the display when you are on the Home Screen looking at the grid view. This will bring up a

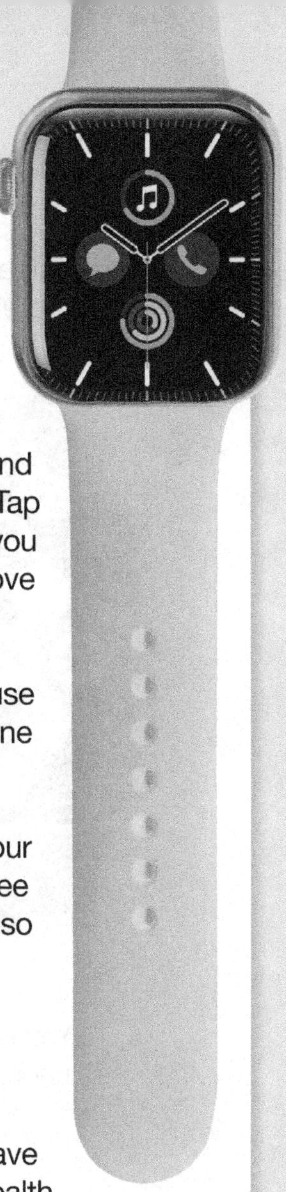

menu with two options: Grid View and List View. Press the List View button, and now your apps will be arranged in an alphabetical list where you can see both the icon and the name of the app.

To remove an app from your **Apple Watch**, open the Home Screen to view the app grid. Touch and hold anywhere on the display to bring up a menu, and choose Edit apps. You will see a small X appear over each of the app icons. Tap the X to delete the app. If you have arranged your apps in the list view, all you need to do is swipe left and then tap the Delete button. This action will remove the app from your **Apple Watch** but not your paired **iPhone**.

To change the settings for any apps installed on your **Apple Watch**, you must use the Watch app on your **iPhone**. Navigate to the list of apps and select the one you want to edit. The options will be different for each app.

To see how much storage space your apps use, open the **Settings app** on your **Apple Watch** and select General. There you will find the Storage settings to see how much space is available and how much space is being used. You can also scroll down to see a breakdown of each app's storage usage.

Default Apps

Your **Apple Watch** comes preloaded with a fantastic series of apps that have been tried and tested. You can safely rely on these apps to improve your health and fitness, keep you up-to-date and productive, and help you stay in touch with friends and family.

These apps include:

Activity

This is the primary activity tracker on the iPhone and Apple Watch, with its characteristic ring design. Each day, your rings will reset, and your daily goal is to complete each one. The purpose of Activity is to get you moving, burn more calories, and spend less time in a static position. See more info about this app in the Health section.

You will be asked if you would like to configure Activity when you first set up your **Apple Watch**, but you can also get started by opening the app. When the app is open, swipe left on the display to see the description of the **Move, Exercise, and Stand rings**. Then tap Get Started. You can set all your personal information, including sex, age, height, weight, and whether or not you use a wheelchair, using the **Digital Crown**. Then all you need to do is select an activity from the list and get moving.

Activity app

You can check on your progress at any time of the day. The app will show you three rings, and each ring will fill up as you move.

- The red, outermost ring is your Move ring and shows you how many calories you have burned.
- The green ring is the Exercise ring, and this tracks how many minutes of brisk exercise you have done.
- The blue, innermost ring is the Stand ring, and this tracks how many times during the 12 hours of the day that you have stood and moved about for at least one minute.

If you are in a wheelchair, the blue Stand ring becomes your Roll ring and will track how many times you have rolled about for at least one minute for every hour of the day. There are a few watch faces to choose from that will display these rings for you, and you can also add complications. You can check your progress, not simply by looking at the rings but also by scrolling through the app, where you can find a progress graph and indicators of your total steps, distance, workouts, and flights of stairs climbed.

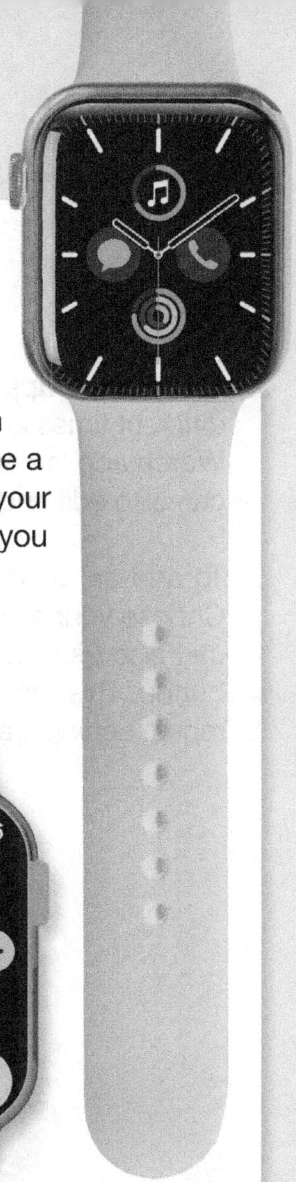

When the rings close, it means you have reached your goal for the day. You can turn the **Digital Crown** while in the app to view your weekly summary.

You can change your daily goals if you find that you are consistently not reaching or exceeding them. Open the Activity app on your **Apple Watch** and use the **Digital Crown** to scroll to the bottom of the screen. You will see a Change Goals button; tap it. Use the [+] and [-] signs to adjust each goal to your liking, then tap Next. Your **Apple Watch** will suggest the optimal goals for you based on your previous performance.

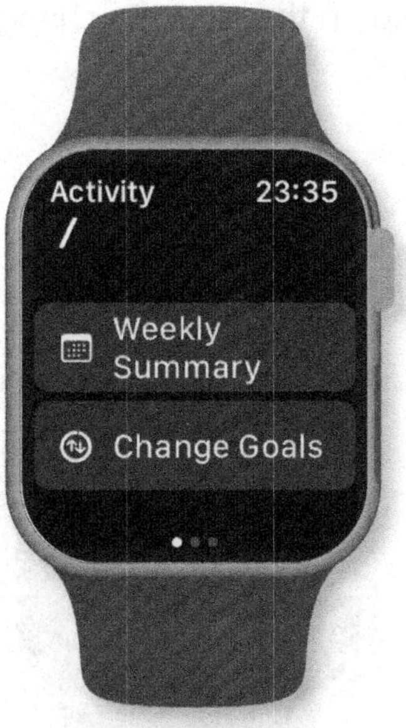

When you consistently close your Activity rings, you can receive awards. This includes awards for personal records, streaks, and major milestones. Open the Activity app on your **Apple Watch** and swipe left twice to see your awards. This will take you to the Awards screen, where you can scroll up and down to see all of the badges you have earned. Tap on any badge to view the details.

Alarms

The **Alarms app** works much like the alarms on your **iPhone**, allowing you to set alarms for different times and periods and giving you the option to snooze or dismiss them. The **Apple Watch** app is connected to your **iPhone** app and will sync with your existing alarms, but you can also edit and add new ones.

To add an alarm on your **Apple Watch**, open the Alarms app. Tap the **Add Alarm button**. Choose your alarm time by setting AM or PM, and then tapping in the hour and minutes. You can also use the **Digital Crown** to set the desired time. When you are done, tap the Check button. This will set the alarm, and you will see it in the Alarm app. Tap on the alarm to change repeat settings, add a label, or customize the snooze options.

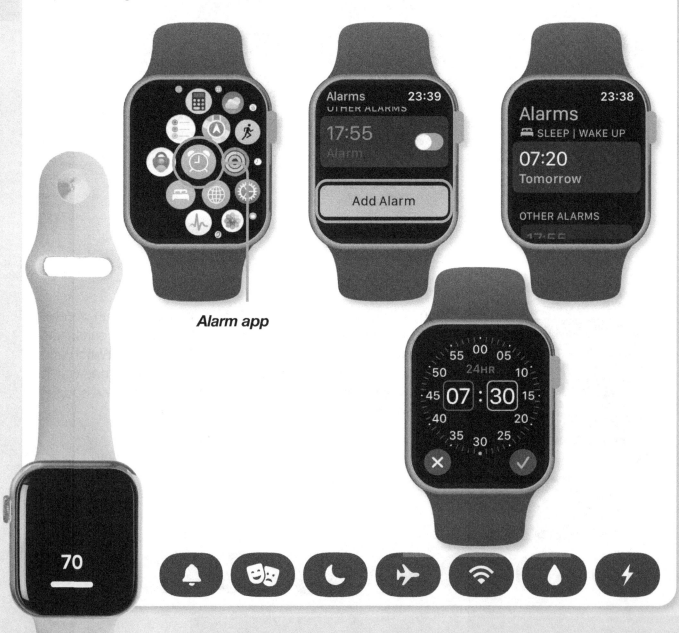

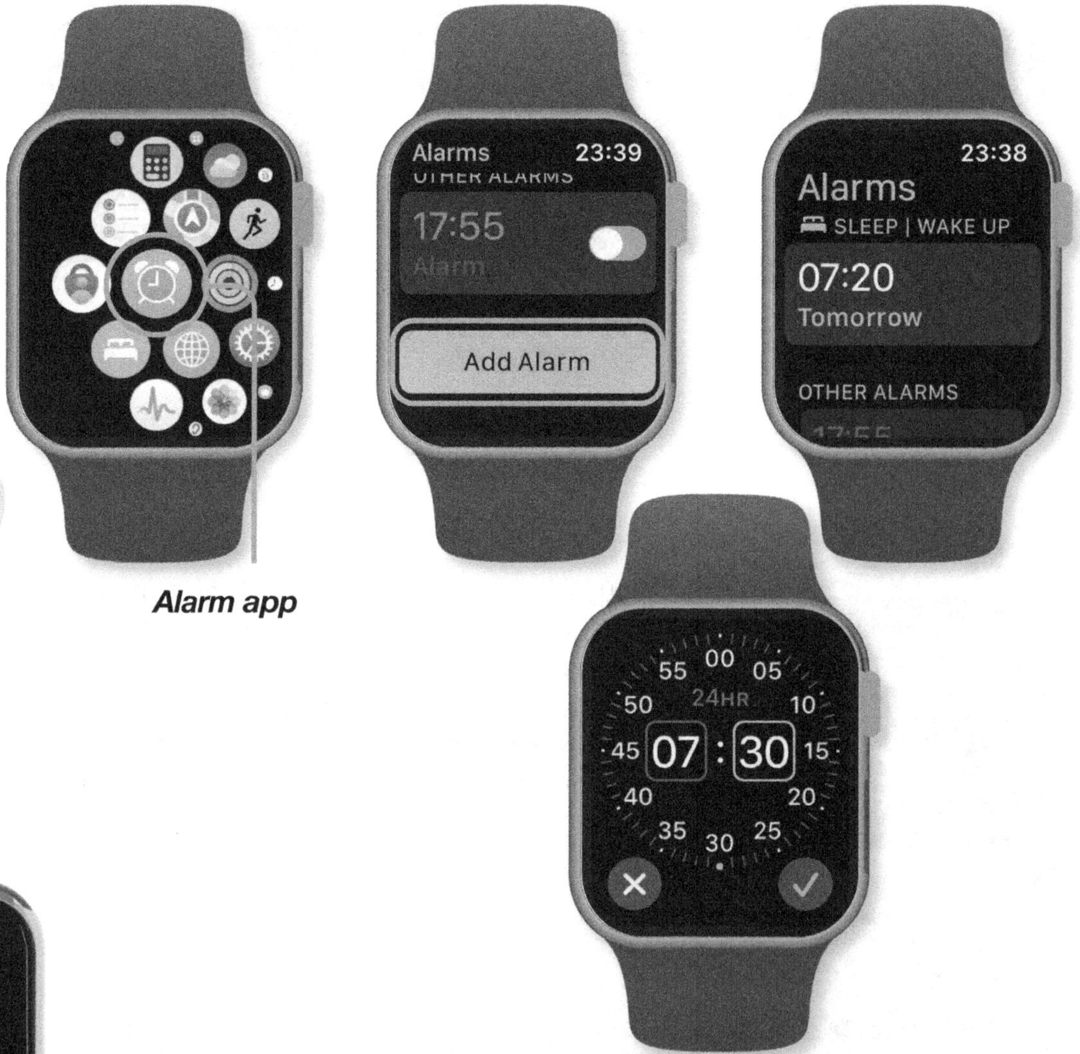

App Store

You can access the App Store through your **Apple Watch** using this app, giving you access to a wide range of compatible apps that can give you the most out of your device.

App Store app

Audiobooks

This app connects you with the Audiobooks subscription-based service that gives you access to over 300,000 titles and millions of podcasts. You must sign up using a computer or your **iPhone**, but once your membership is active, you can use the **Apple Watch** app to listen to all your favorite content. Audiobooks offers pricing options to suit your needs and give you access to new releases and best sellers.

Audiobooks app

Blood Oxygen

Get an on-demand reading of your blood oxygen levels, which indicates how well your blood can transport oxygen from your lungs to the rest of your body. This is especially useful in an era where respiratory diseases have reached pandemic levels, impacting the ability of people to breathe properly. Find more information about this app in the Health section.

Calculator

This is a standard calculator that you can use for simple math problems. The **Apple Watch** version of this app does not include a scientific calculator and only the basic functions of [+], [-], [÷], and [×].

Calendar

This app connects with the Calendar app on your **iPhone** to see all your upcoming events and schedule new ones.

Camera remote

Use your **Apple Watch** as a remote for the camera on your **iPhone** to easily take pictures from a distance. All you need to do is set up the Camera app on your **iPhone**, and then you can use your **Apple Watch** to take the picture once you are in the frame. You can also set a timer so you don't capture yourself looking at your wrist. The Camera remote also works with Siri, so you can speak out loud instead of pressing a button even if you are not close to your **iPhone**'s microphone.

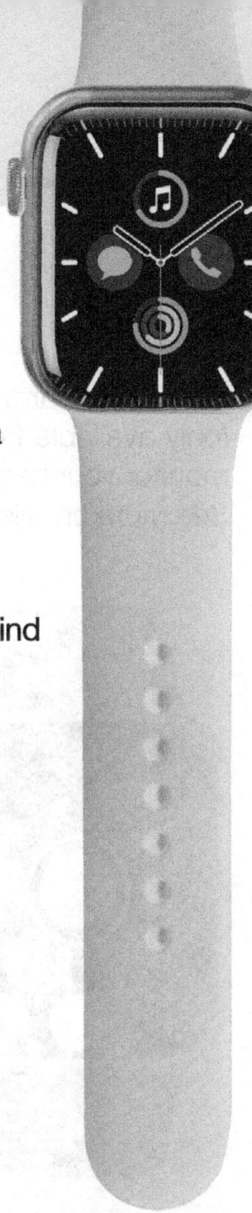

Compass

Use your compass to navigate and orientate yourself, as it shows you which way North is. By default, the compass will indicate magnetic North, like a standard compass, though you can change it to show True North instead.

Contacts

This app will sync with the Contacts app on your **iPhone** so you can always find a phone number or email address.

Phone app

Cycle Tracking

A tailor-made app that helps track your menstrual cycle. This is useful for monitoring your health and tracking symptoms, even those associated with menopause. You can use Cycle Tracking to monitor your fertile periods and identify any patterns of concern. Cycle Tracking is also useful for monitoring other health symptoms, such as headaches, which might have a particular trigger

Cycle Tracking app

ECG

The Electrocardiogram app is a flagship feature of the **Apple Watch** (only available from Series 4 onwards), allowing you to see and monitor your heart rhythm while looking out for any irregularities. See more on this app in the Health section.

ECG app

Find Devices

You can use your **Apple Watch** to find any of the Apple devices connected to your Apple ID as long as you have enabled the Find My service. When activated, this app will use GPS to lead you to your lost device, whether you accidentally lost your **iPhone** while working in the garden, or you managed to get your iPad hidden amongst your magazine collection.

Find Devices app

Find Items

Similar to Find Devices, this app is used to locate items that you have marked with an Apple AirTag.

Find Items app

This tag connects to a GPS signal, and you can attach it to any item, from your dog's collar to your luggage. For someone who never remembers where they parked their car in the parking lot, this could be a real godsend!

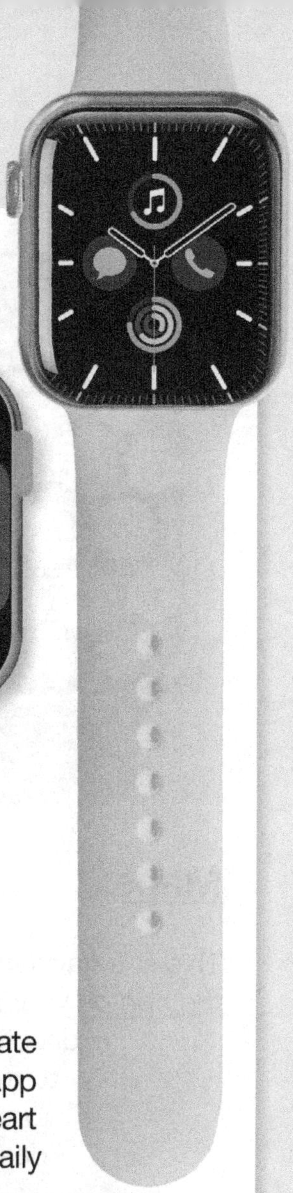

Find People

Keep track of where your loved ones are, as long as they have enabled location sharing with you. Make sure that your friends and family arrive home safely or follow their journey as they travel overseas.

Find Items app

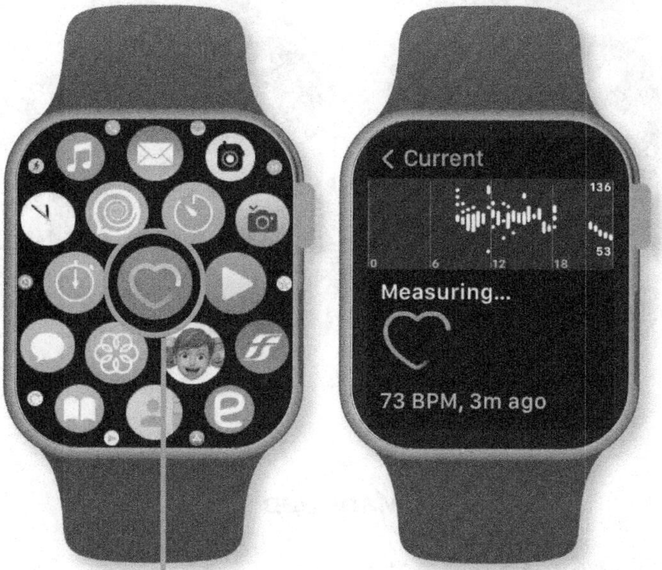

Heart Rate app

Heart Rate

Keep track of your heart rate throughout the day. This app shows you your current heart rate and calculates your daily average resting heart rate.

Home app

Home

Use your **Apple Watch** to control your HomeKit accessories such as light switches, doorbells, thermostats, switches, sprinklers, security cameras, etc.

Mail

This is a companion app for the Mail app on your **iPhone** and other Apple devices that you can use to read and reply to your emails.

Mail app

Maps

This is a navigation app that works with the app on your **iPhone** to help you find directions and can give you turn-by-turn instructions to help you reach your destination. The app can also include live traffic data to help you avoid congestion and find the quickest routes.

and find the quickest routes.

Maps app

Memoji

With this app, you can create a custom emoji that looks just like you or your friends and family. Save the emojis in your sticker collection so that you can send them in any message or email.

Memoji app

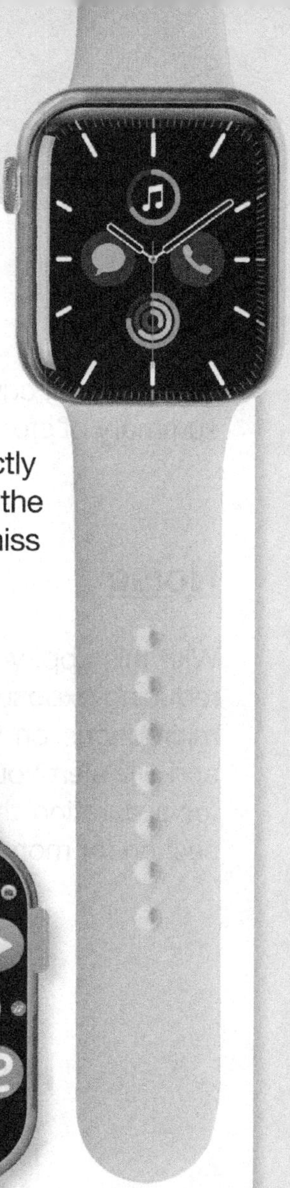

Messages

View and reply to your texts and iMessages directly on your **Apple Watch**. This app will sync with the Messages app on your **iPhone** so you'll never miss any communication.

Messagges app

Mindfulness

With this app, you can beat stress by setting aside a few dedicated minutes to breathing, calming, and focusing your mind. Find more info about this app in the Health section.

Mindfulness app

Music

This is a companion app that works with the version on your **iPhone**, allowing you to download and sync selected content directly onto your **Apple Watch**, allowing you to listen to it at any time. The Music app works best with a Bluetooth headset.

Music app

News

See the most current and relevant news stories directly on your **Apple Watch**. Scroll through a summary of stories and select articles to read in full without needing to use your **iPhone**.

Noise

With this app, you can help protect and prolong your hearing by reducing exposure to very loud noises. The Noise app uses the microphone on your **Apple Watch** to measure ambient sound and will alert you when you have been exposed to loud noises for a duration that may cause damage. See the Health focus section for more information.

Noise app

Now Playing

This app allows you to control the playback of any media apps on your **iPhone**, **Apple Watch**, or other Apple devices. Use it to pause, play, skip forward, or back on an audiobook, podcast, video, or song.

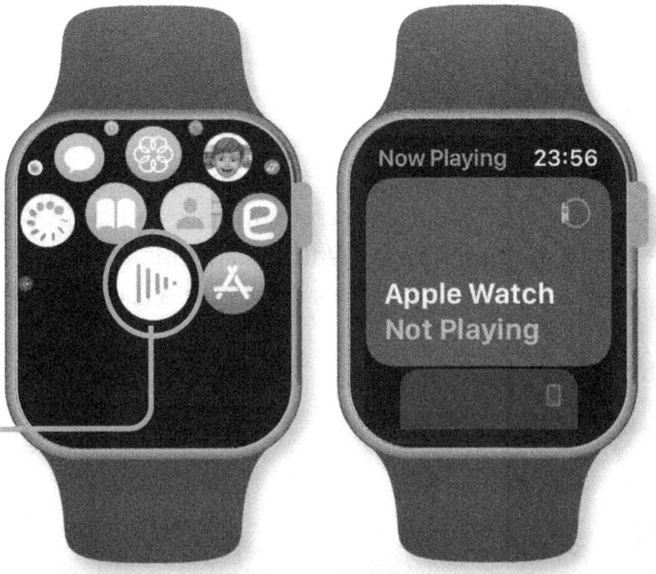

Now Playing app

Phone

Answer or make a phone call. This app works through your **iPhone** to connect you with your contacts through a voice call.

Phone app

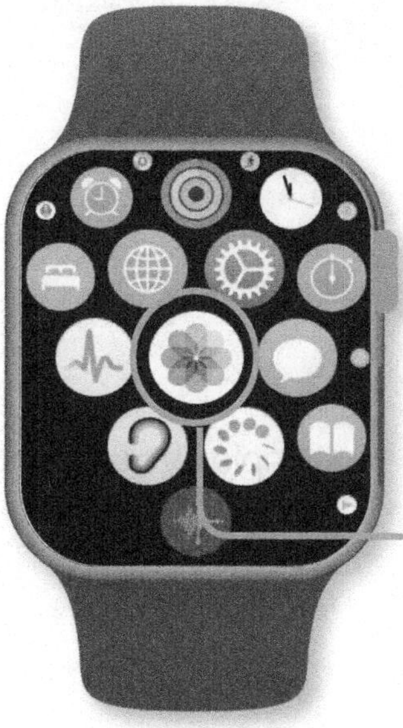

Photos app

Photos

View selected albums directly on your **Apple Watch** with the Photos app. You can choose which albums to sync using the Photos app on your **iPhone**.

Podcasts

Listen to an almost unlimited number of podcasts and download them to your **Apple Watch**. The app offers pause, play, skip forward, and backward controls.

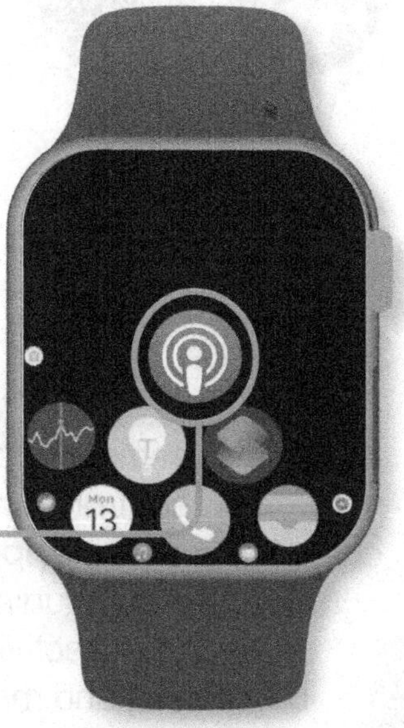

Podcasts app

Reminders

This is a companion app that works with the version on your **iPhone** to keep track of and get alerts for all your important reminders. You can also create reminders using your **Apple Watch** and dismiss any alerts received.

Reminders app

Remote

This app allows you to control your Apple TV using your **Apple Watch**.

Remote app

Settings

All of the settings you need to control and customize your **Apple Watch**, including display, connectivity, brightness, and more.

Settings app

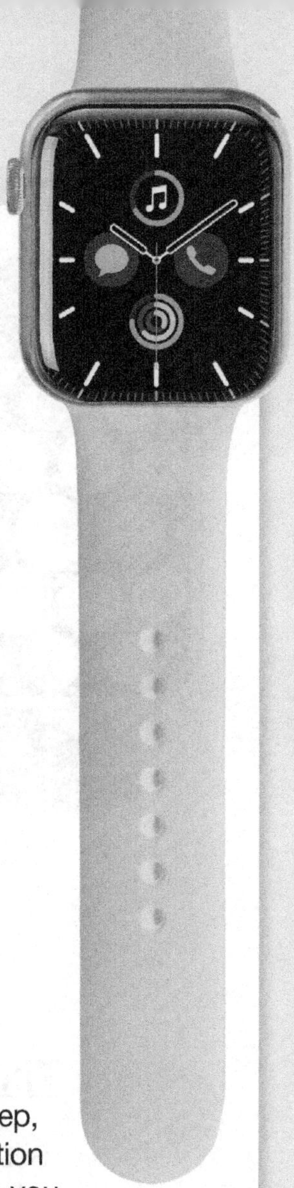

Sleep app

Sleep

Monitor your sleep, including the duration and quality, to ensure you are getting enough rest. Set sleep goals and generate reports to identify any disturbances that you can remove to improve your overall quality of sleep.

Stocks

Monitoring stocks on your **Apple Watch** means you'll never miss a lucrative investment or miss any major shortfalls. You can choose which stocks you want to see on your **Apple Watch**.

Stopwatch/Timer app

Stopwatch

Use this app on your **Apple Watch** to time events and track laps easily and efficiently.

Timer

Set a countdown timer to alert you when it runs out directly on your wrist.

Stopwatch/Timer app

Voice Memos

Use your **Apple Watch** to record a short voice memo that you can refer back to at any time using your **iPhone** or **Apple Watch**. This is a more useful way of keeping notes on your **Apple Watch**, where it can be difficult to type something out on a keyboard.

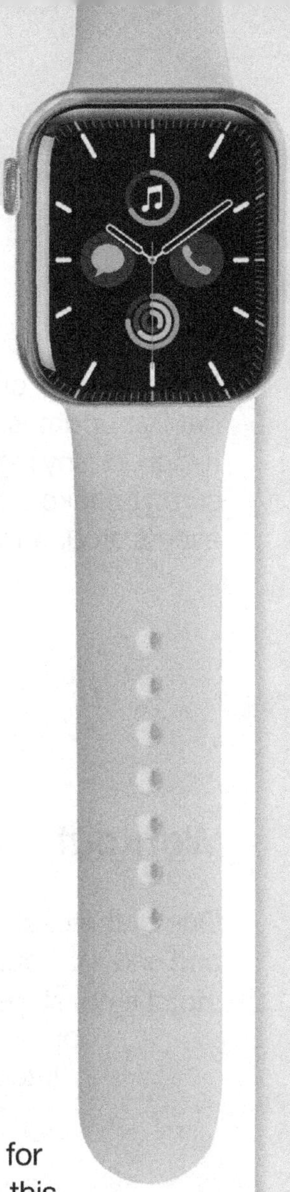

Walkie-Talkie

This is a companion to the FaceTime app, which you can use to talk with friends. If you both have FaceTime installed and have added each other as a contact on the Walkie-Talkie app, you can instantly connect and chat.

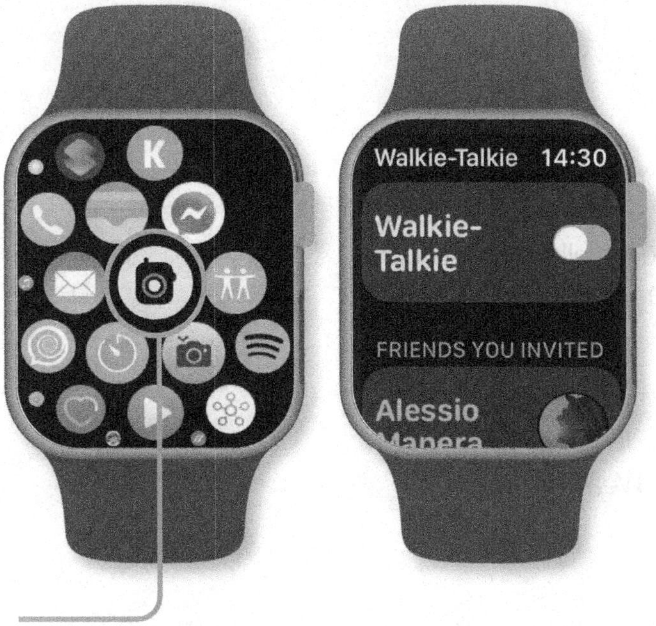

Walkie takie app

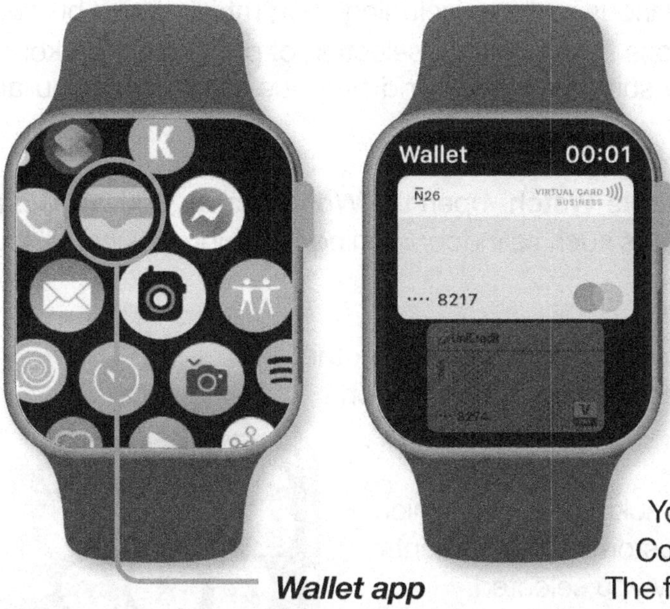

Wallet app

Wallet

A companion app for Wallet on the **iPhone**, this allows you to scan your watch and pay for goods or services. Your **Apple Watch** must have a passcode enabled to use this feature to protect your sensitive banking details.

You can use Wallet to store and display your Covid-19 vaccination card if you have one. The first step is to scane the QR code povided on your proof of vaccination with your **iPhone** camera. This will direct you to a link where you can download the vaccination record to the Wallet and Health apps on your phone. You will be able to view your vaccination record on your **iPhone** by double-pressing the side button, or on your **Apple Watch** by double-pressing the side button and scrolling down to the vaccination card, which should be located after all of your bank cards.

Weather

Use this app on your **Apple Watch** to get live updates on the weather in your region, or any region in the world. Make sure you take an umbrella or plan your events around the weather.

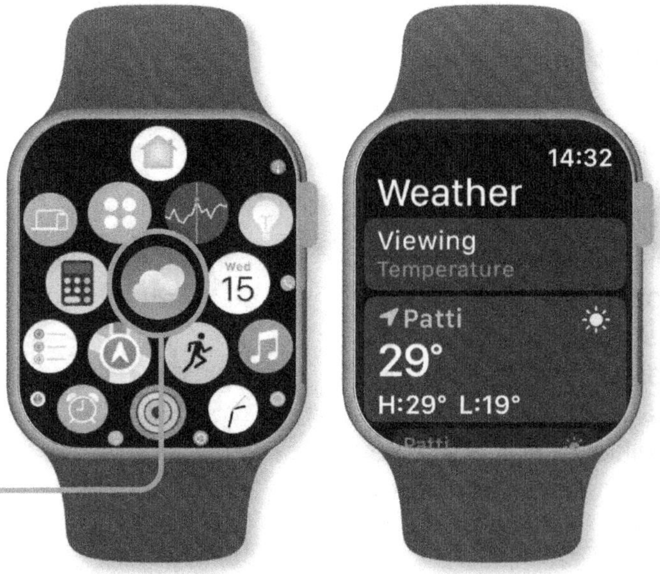

Weather app

Workout

One of the best features of the **Apple Watch** is the Workout app. Use it to start, track, pause, and end workout sessions while tracking various metrics, including heart rate, calories burned, total time, steps, and pace. You can choose from the large selection of predefined workouts or create a custom workout to suit your needs and produce the metrics you are interested in seeing.

To start a workout on your **Apple Watch**, open the Workout app. You will find a list of preprogrammed workouts such as indoor running, outdoor walking, hiking, pilates, and more.

Use the **Digital Crown** or swipe up and down on the display to scroll through these options and select one by tapping on it.

This will open the workout tracking screen, which will show you a series of custom measurements that are relevant to the activity you selected.

For example, if you select outdoor running, you will see distance, elapsed time, and pace. If you select swimming, you will see a lap counter. If you select an activity like yoga, you will see elapsed time, calories burned, and heart rate.

Workout app

You can also add a custom workout goal by scrolling to the bottom of the list and selecting Add Workout. Here you can name your workout and select which parameters to include, such as calories, time, distance, etc.

When you are ready to begin a custom or preinstalled workout, tap the Start button.

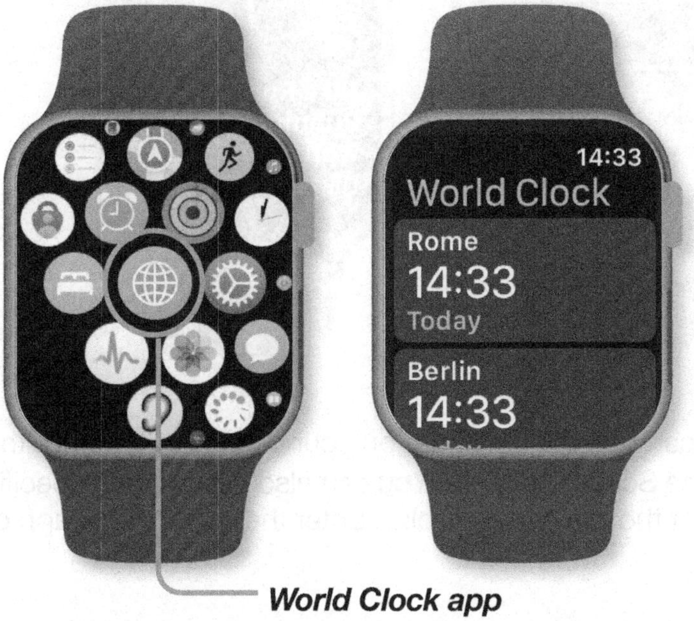

World Clock app

World Clock

Set your favorite locations to see the time anywhere in the world using your **Apple Watch**.

Finding New Apps

Along with the helpful apps that come standard with your **Apple Watch** you can also choose from thousands of third-party apps available to you through the App Store.

- Open the **App Store** on your **Apple Watch**.
- Use the **Digital Crown** to browse through the apps that are featured on the front page.
- **Tap the Get button to download the app onto your Apple Watch.** You will be asked to confirm your download by double-pressing the side button.

- If the app is not free, you will see a price in place of the Get button. Tap on this price to complete a purchase before the download can proceed.

- If you have previously downloaded the app but since removed it, you will see a cloud icon. Tap this icon to reinstall the app on your device.

If you have a Series 7 you can use the keyboard on your display to type out the text, or use dictate or the Scribble feature. You can also search for a specific app using the search bar at the top of the display. Enter the name of the app or keyword to search for it.

Another option to easily download apps onto your **Apple Watch** is to use your **iPhone.** Simply open the Watch app and select the App Store tab, which you can find at the bottom of the screen. You will be directed to a page on the App Store exclusively for **Apple Watch** apps.

Health Focus

has come a long way since its first appearance on the

The **Apple Watch** has come a long way since its first appearance on the market, where it was touted as a Smartwatch with comprehensive features to improve and track fitness. Today, the Apple Watch is the forerunner in health and wellness monitoring, helping to keep you in the loop regarding your health stats and actually save lives. From detecting and alerting you to

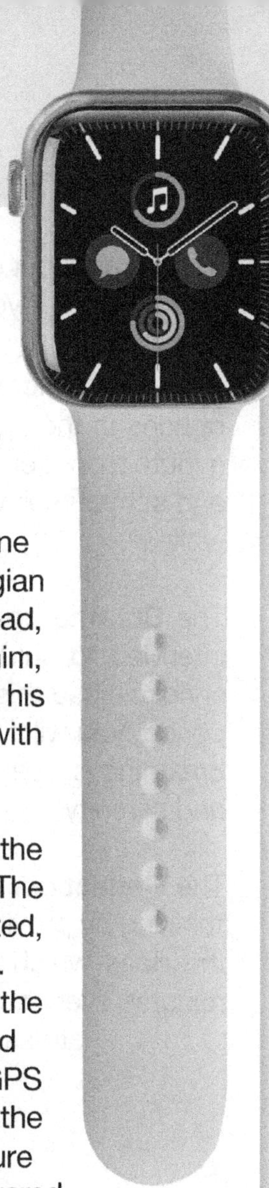

an irregular heart rhythm so that you can seek medical attention fast, giving you an easy way to make an emergency call when you cannot access your phone, or letting your contacts know when you have fallen down or taken an impact, the **Apple Watch** can be a true guardian to keep you safe. All of these improvements make the **Apple Watch** useful not only for the young, fit, and highly active but also for older generations.

You can find many stories about how the Apple Watch became a lifesaver. One harrowing example is the experience of Toralv Østvang—a 68-year-old Norwegian man. Toralv recalls waking up in bed one morning with immense pain in his head, and his face was covered in blood. He had no idea what had happened to him, with little recollection of the night's events. As he slowly started to regain his senses, he realized he was surrounded by three policemen, staring at him with concern on their faces.

His **Apple Watch** told the story of what happened: sometime around 4 am, the Sleep app showed that he had arisen from bed and headed to the bathroom. The Heart Rate monitoring features showed that his heart rate suddenly plummeted, causing him to faint and land face-first on the hard tiles of the bathroom floor. Somehow, he made his way back to bed, though he lost all recollection of the incident. Luckily, his **Apple Watch** detected the fall and immediately notified emergency services, who were able to rush down to the home thanks to the GPS coordinates being sent from the device. You can see how several features of the **Apple Watch** worked together to help Toralv put the pieces together and figure out exactly what happened. Not only could he understand why he awoke covered in blood, but emergency services were already present, and he didn't even need to make a phone call in his dazed state. (Orellana, 2020)

Hopefully, you do not share a similar experience, but you can rest assured that if something does go wrong, your **Apple Watch** will be there for you. Let's take a look at some of the health features offered on your device.

Mindfulness

Taking care of our mental health is underappreciated and not always easy. The Mindfulness app, released on watchOS 8, is a new and improved version of its predecessor, the Breathe app, and is intended to help you find more calm and focus in your life by removing distractions and letting you sit in a quiet place with your own thoughts for just a few minutes each day. These meditative practices have been proven to help improve mental health by reducing anxiety and depression, allowing you to eliminate stressful thoughts and bring your body into a state of relaxation. Combating stress is not only good for the mind but also for the body, and you can slowly fight back against aches, pains, and inflammation if you take the time to de-stress.

The Mindfulness App offers two choices: Breathe or Reflect. When you select one of these options in the app, you will then need to choose a duration ranging anywhere from just one minute to longer sessions of up to 30 minutes or more. Make sure to read through the prompts and set yourself up in a comfortable and safe environment where you can be alone for a short while.

The **Breathe** option will show you an animation and provide haptic feedback on your wrist intended to guide the pace of your breathing. You will see a shape that slowly grows and shrinks—use this to time your breaths. By following this breathing pattern, even for a short period, you will find that your thoughts become calmer and your heart rate slows down. Deep breathing is an ancient method used by so many cultures across the world to bring more peace and serenity.

The **Reflect** option in the Mindfulness app is intended to guide you to a more positive way of thinking by providing you with different prompts to consider. Take a few minutes to think about the ideas, which often include themes of gratitude and positive aspirations. Doing this for a few minutes every day can help you develop more empathy for others and yourself, reducing your stress levels and contributing to a fuller and more enjoyable life.

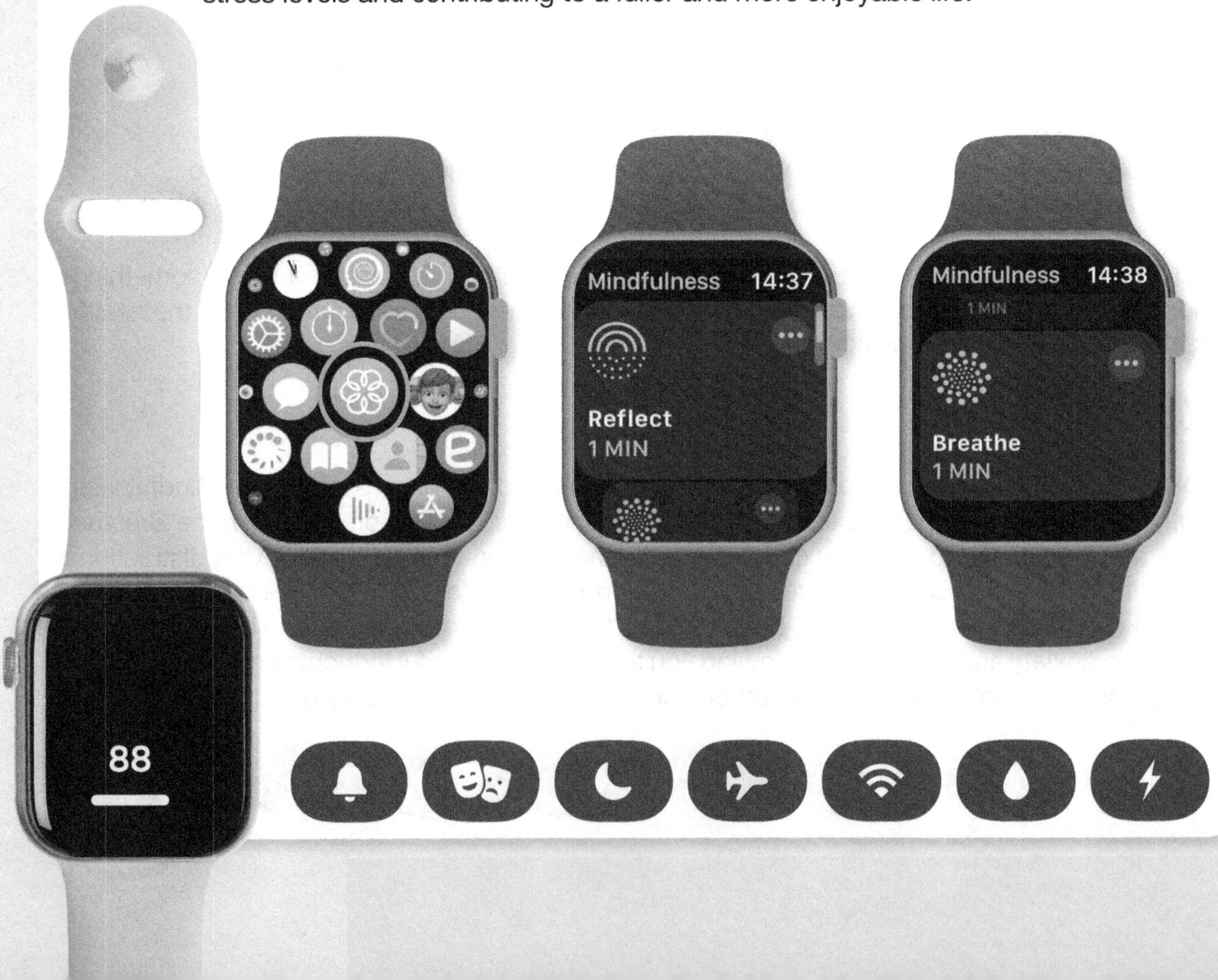

At the end of each Breathe or Reflect session, you will receive a haptic alert on your wrist to let you know that the timer has ended, and a short report on how your heart rate was impacted. This is a good way of keeping track of your own progress in managing and monitoring your mental health and its impacts on your body.

You can enable notifications from the Mindfulness app so that you never miss a Breathe or Reflect session.

Sleep

Getting enough sleep is critical to good health, and far too many people ignore this, prioritizing other things instead of their rest. With the Sleep app on your **Apple Watch**, you can begin to develop healthier and more consistent sleep patterns that will help your body to recover fully and leave you feeling rested when you wake up.

Use the Sleep app to create a bedtime schedule by setting your wake-up time and desired sleep goal. Through the app, you can set alarms to wake you up in the morning, and it will also tell you what time you should go to bed in order to meet your sleep goals. Easily choose alarm tones and select which days you need to stick to a sleep schedule. For example, most people only worry about going to bed on time during the week and take a more relaxed approach on the weekends.

The app includes a wind-down period about half an hour before your bedtime to help you develop a healthy routine that promotes good sleep. During your wind-down time, you should try to limit your screen time. As you sleep, your **Apple Watch** will track your sleep, monitoring how much you toss and turn to determine the quality of your sleep and calculating how many hours of sleep you get. The Sleep app monitors your respiratory rate by measuring how often you breathe to provide more insights into the quality of your sleep, looking out for different periods such as light sleep, deep sleep, and REM.

Easily view all of your sleep records through the Sleep app on your **iPhone**, where you can see the details of your bedtime schedule, sleep goals, average time spent in bed, and average time asleep.

- To change any settings on your **Apple Watch**, open the **Settings app** and scroll to the **Sleep options:**

◊ Turn on at **Wind Down**: this feature will enable Sleep Focus mode, which reduces your notifications and alerts so that your phone becomes less distracting and you can begin reducing your screen time.

◊ **Sleep Screen**: shows a simplified display on your **Apple Watch** and **iPhone** lock screen when this is enabled. This feature helps to reduce distractions.

◊ **Show Time**: enable this feature to show the date and time on your **Apple Watch** and **iPhone** when in Sleep Focus mode.

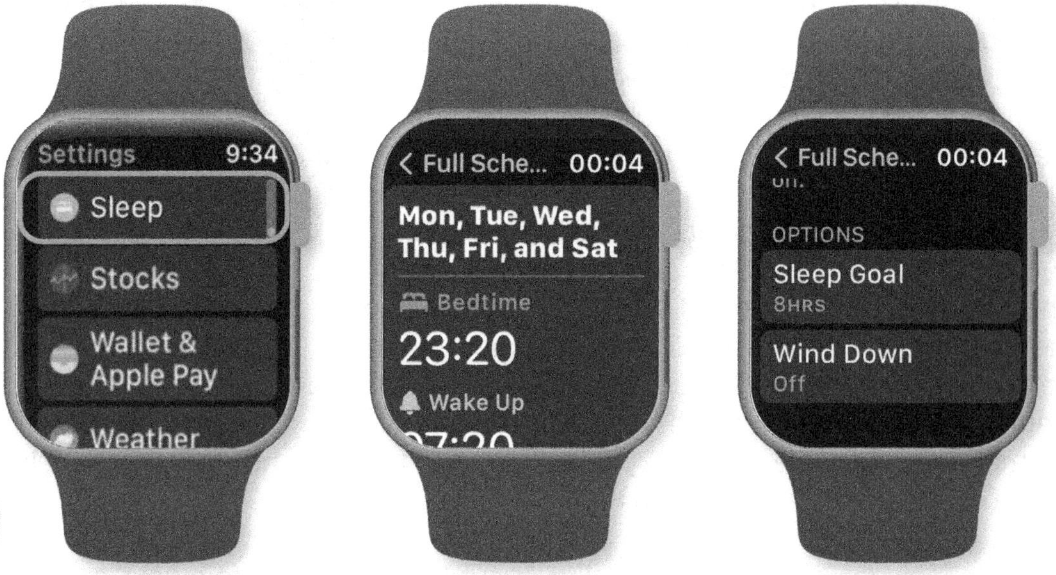

- Change notification settings such as sleep tracking and charge reminders. If enabled, your watch can remind you to charge it before your wind-down time begins so that you can track your sleep through the night.

- These settings can also be accessed through the Sleep app on your **iPhone**.

Handwashing

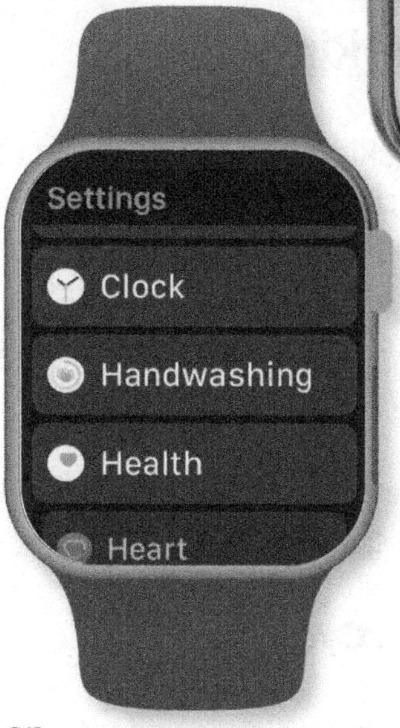

To promote good hygiene practices and per recommendations made by the World Health Organization, you can enable a feature on your **Apple Watch** that will detect when you begin to wash your hands and help to encourage you to clean them for at least 20 seconds. Not only that, but the Handwashing feature can also remind you to wash your hands when you arrive home. Handwashing has shown significant benefits in reducing the spread of germs and in helping to combat global pandemics. (Alzyood et al., 2020)

- To turn on Handwashing, open the **Settings app** on your **Apple Watch**.

- Scroll down to Handwashing, and enable the **Handwashing timer.**

- You can enable or disable Handwashing notifications and reminder in these settings.

You can see an interesting report of your average handwashing times using your **iPhone**:

- Open the **Health app** on your **iPhone.**

- Select **Browse**, and then select **Other Data**.

- Here you can see an option for Handwashing.

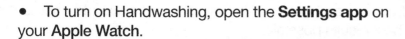

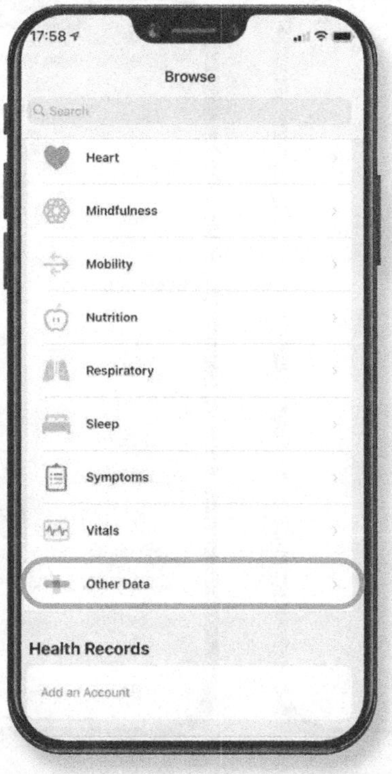

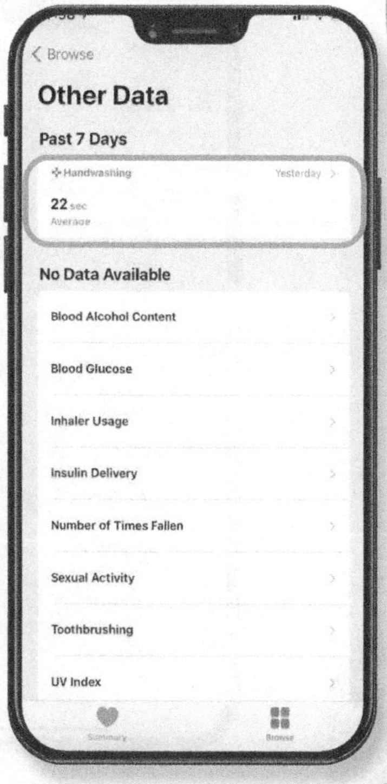

Cycle Tracking

The Cycle Tracking app is designed to help you track your menstrual cycle, allowing you to log symptoms and predict the onset of your next period. Of course, not everybody will find this app useful; it is targeted toward a specific niche group.

- To get started with the Cycle Tracking app on your **Apple Watch**, begin by opening the Health app on your **iPhone**.
- Tap the **Browse tab** at the bottom of the display, which will direct you to a list of various health categories.
- Choose **Cycle Tracking.**
- Follow the on-screen instructions and enter all the relevant information to ensure the app can provide you with the best results possible.
- Tap the **Options button** to change your notification settings, heart rate data, and period and fertility predictions.

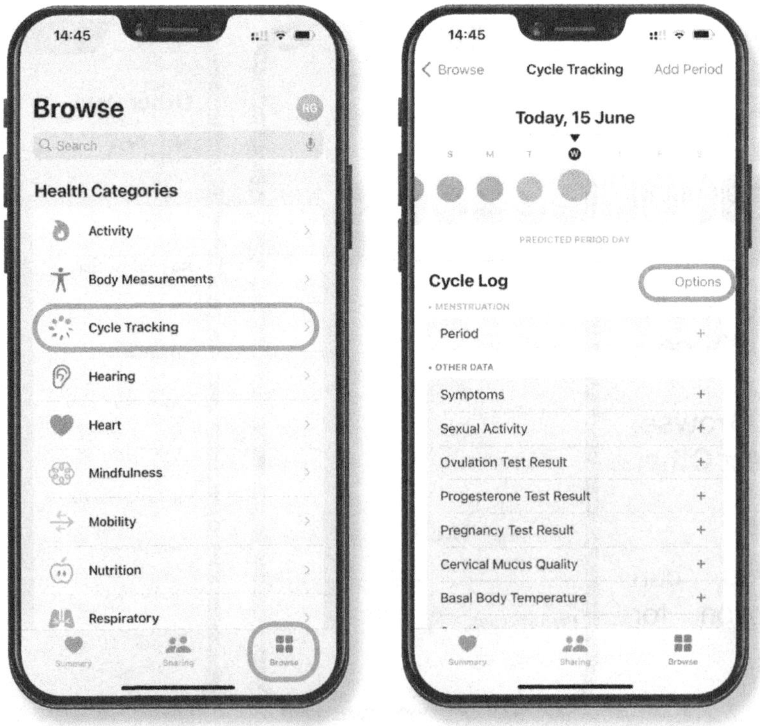

Once you have the app set up, you can begin to log your cycle using your **Apple Watch.**

- Open the **Cycle Tracking** app on your **Apple Watch.**
- You will see a calendar view showing today's date, and you can scroll across the screen to see previous or upcoming dates.
- Tap on the dates to begin logging any symptoms.
- The app will use your data to generate predictions about when your next cycle is set to begin.

By using the Health app on your **iPhone**, you can easily choose what kind of notifications you would like to receive from the Cycle Tracking app.

- Choose **Cycle Tracking** from the **Browse tab** in the **Health app**.
- Scroll down until you see Options.
- Here you can choose to enable or disable period predictions, period notifications, fertility predictions, fertility notifications, and heart rate data.

Noise Detection

Protect your hearing with the Noise app on your **Apple Watch.** This app measures ambient sounds and will alert you if you are exposed to noise over a chosen decibel threshold or if the average noise level is very high for more than three minutes.

Long-term exposure to loud sounds can impair your hearing over time, and the louder the noise, the less time it can take to cause hearing loss. Prolonged exposure can cause permanent damage. Sounds below 80 decibels are usually safe and should not damage your hearing. However, as sounds begin to approach 85, 90, or 95 decibels, it takes only 2 hours to 10 minutes to cause temporary hearing loss. Any sound louder than 100 decibels will cause damage to your hearing, even if you are only exposed for a few minutes.

- To set up the **Noise app,** begin by opening it on your **Apple Watch.**

- To turn on noise monitoring, tap the **enable button.**

- Make sure you have Noise notifications enabled so that your Apple Watch can alert you when noise levels become dangerous:

- Open the **Health app** on your **iPhone**. Tap the **My Watch tab** at the bottom of the display.

- Scroll to **Noise**.

- Here you can select a **noise threshold**. When noise levels exceed this level, you will receive an alert.

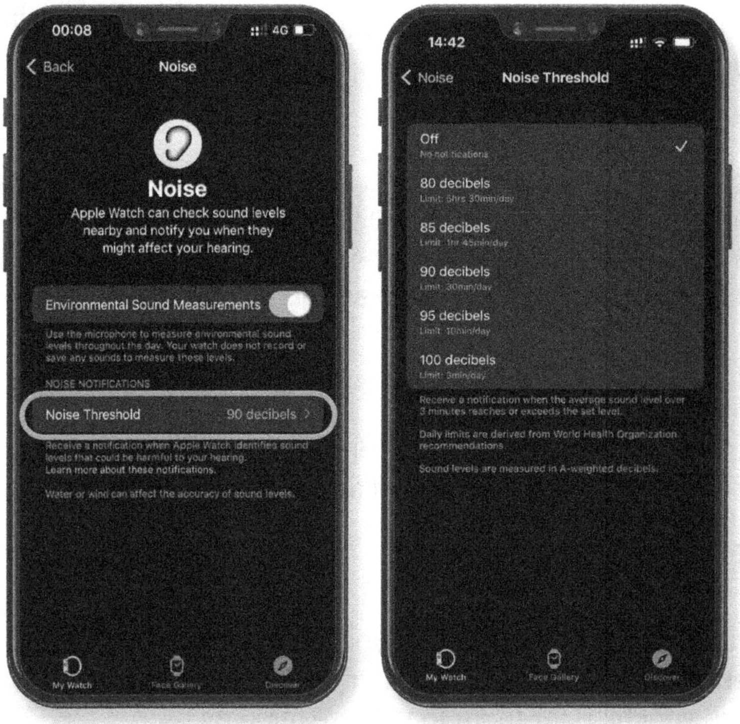

You can use the Noise app on your **Apple Watch** to measure noise levels. Open the app, and it will give you a decibel reading of your environment.

The Noise app can also be used for different types of situations. If you are lucky enough to watch the launch of a spacecraft, you may be interested in measuring the sound level during takeoff. Or while visiting the zoo, it can be interesting to measure how many decibels a lion produces when it roars.

A Frisco, Texas man, Scott Bennet, 59, retold his experience using the noise detection feature on his **Apple Watch**. His son, Sam, was diagnosed with autism, and though he thrived on social interaction and had many good relationships, one thing that he did struggle with was finding his 'inside voice'. He was unable to modulate it appropriately, leading to many uncomfortable and unfortunate situations. The family had tried everything they could to get Sam speaking to people at a normal volume, but though he would do so when asked, it would only be for a short time before returning to his usual, and very loud, voice. Scott showed his son how his speaking alerted the **Apple Watch** Noise detection app of very loud noises that could potentially lead to hearing damage. Sam was quite amused but began to understand that his volume levels were harming those around him. The **Apple Watch** helped this family lead a slightly quieter life with more peaceful interactions (DeSantis, 2019).

Heart Rate Monitor

You can use your **Apple Watch** as a non-invasive way of monitoring your heart health. It can be a valuable tool in identifying any irregularities that might warrant a trip to the doctor. Remember that the **Apple Watch** is not a medical device and should not be relied on to diagnose severe heart conditions.

Use your **Apple Watch** to check your heart rate by opening the app on your device. You will be able to view your:

- **Resting heart rate**: how fast your heart beats when you are not doing any physical activity. A regular resting heart rate can fall anywhere between 60 to 100 beats per minute, though many factors can impact this number. Your **Apple Watch** will collect your resting heart rate data over time and produce an average. With this average, you will be able to identify if you are experiencing unusually high or low heart rates.

- **Walking heart rate:** one way to measure how your heart responds to mild exercise. When you walk, your heart rate will naturally increase as it begins to pump more blood and oxygen throughout the body. You can use this as a general indicator of physical fitness, and the expected range is quite broad, spanning anywhere from 60 to 120 beats per minute. You should always consider your average when looking at walking heart rate.

- **Breathe rate:** Your breathing rate is related to your heart rate during Breathe sessions which you can access through the Mindfulness app. The aim here is to reduce your heart rate during a Breathe session to help you calm your mind and body. Your Breathe rate should be quite low, close to your resting heart rate, though sometimes even lower.

- **Recovery rate:** This is one of the best indicators of physical fitness.

Your recovery rate is taken after you have completed a workout or after your heart rate has spiked and measures how many beats per minute your heart rate decreases in a minute. If you are reasonably fit, you will recover quickly, and your recovery heart rate should be about 20 beats per minute. Anything less than 12 beats per minute may be a concern and indicates that you should spend more time doing physical activity.

- **Workout heart rate:** how fast your heart beats during more strenuous exercise. Your maximum heart rate is generally calculated by subtracting your age from 220, so a 65-year-old would have a maximum heart rate of 155. This means that they can aim to get their workout heart rate anywhere from 65-80% of their maximum during exercise, which would be anywhere between 100 and 124 beats per minute. This will help to keep your heart healthy and strong. However, a person's maximum heart rate can vary significantly from the prescribed calculation, though it generally decreases with age. It is normal for athletic people to get very close to their maximum heart rates or even exceed them during intense exercise. It is not a point of concern unless there are problems recovering and bringing the heart rate back down to resting levels. For older people, it is usually unnecessary to strive to raise your heart rate so much, and you will get benefits from working out at around 65% of your maximum.

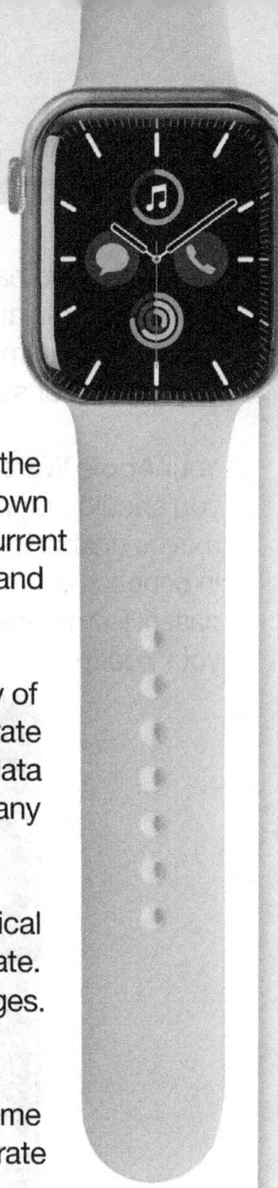

Open the Heart Rate app to view your heart rate data on your **Apple Watch**. You will be able to see your current heart rate. Use the **Digital Crown** or swipe the display up and down to see your resting rate, walking average, recovery rate, and workout heart rate.

You can also view this data on your **iPhone** in some greater detail. Visit the **Health app** and tap the **Browse tab** in the lower part of the display. Scroll down to **Heart** from the menu. You will find a few different tabs showing you the current day's readings, including your current heart rate, variability, resting heart rate, and walking heart rate average.

Below Today's readings, you can find some older heart rate data. Tap on any of these tabs to visually see the history: access graphs showing your heart rate data. Tap the H, D, W, M, and Y buttons at the top of the screen to see your data over hours, days, weeks, months, and years. These periods help identify any changes, improvements, or deterioration in your heart rate averages.

Use the long-term view, like months or years, to see if undertaking regular physical exercise has lowered your average heart rate or improved your recovery rate. Use the shorter periods like hours or days to identify specific events or changes.

Below the graphs are Highlights where you can find important observations and summaries of your heart rate data. The Health app will also provide some interesting insights and information to help you better understand the heart rate data that you should pay attention to.

Heart Health Notifications

You can enable several important heart rate notifications so that your **Apple Watch** can alert you when anything out of the ordinary is detected. This includes unusually high or low heart rates and irregular heart rhythms.

When looking out for unexpectedly low or high heart rates, your **Apple Watch** will consider your activity level. It will not send you an alert about your elevated heart rate if you have just done some exercise, and similarly, you will not be notified about a low heart rate if you are sleeping and your heart rate naturally slows down. You can also receive notifications if your watch detects any irregular heart rhythms, whch may indicate arterial fibrillation.

Irregularities in your heart rate can occur more often as you get older, though it is not always something to be too concerned about. Some people may experience sudden bursts of rapid heart rate, heart palpitations, feelings of fatigue, and shortness of breath. These symptoms may pass after a few minutes or persist, leading to more severe complications and a heart attack or stroke. You must speak to a doctor if you experience any of these symptoms and only use your **Apple Watch** as a supplementary monitor in addition to your doctor's advice, a healthy diet, regular exercise, and listening to how you feel.

Your **Apple Watch** cannot be used to detect a heart attack, so if you experience any symptoms, you should contact medical services or an emergency contact immediately. Your **Apple Watch** maybe unable to detect some irregularities in your heart rate, and you will not receive a notification. In contrast, you may receive a notification about a perfectly normal change in heart rate in other cases. Remember, your **Apple Watch** is not a medical device; it can only assist you in managing your health.

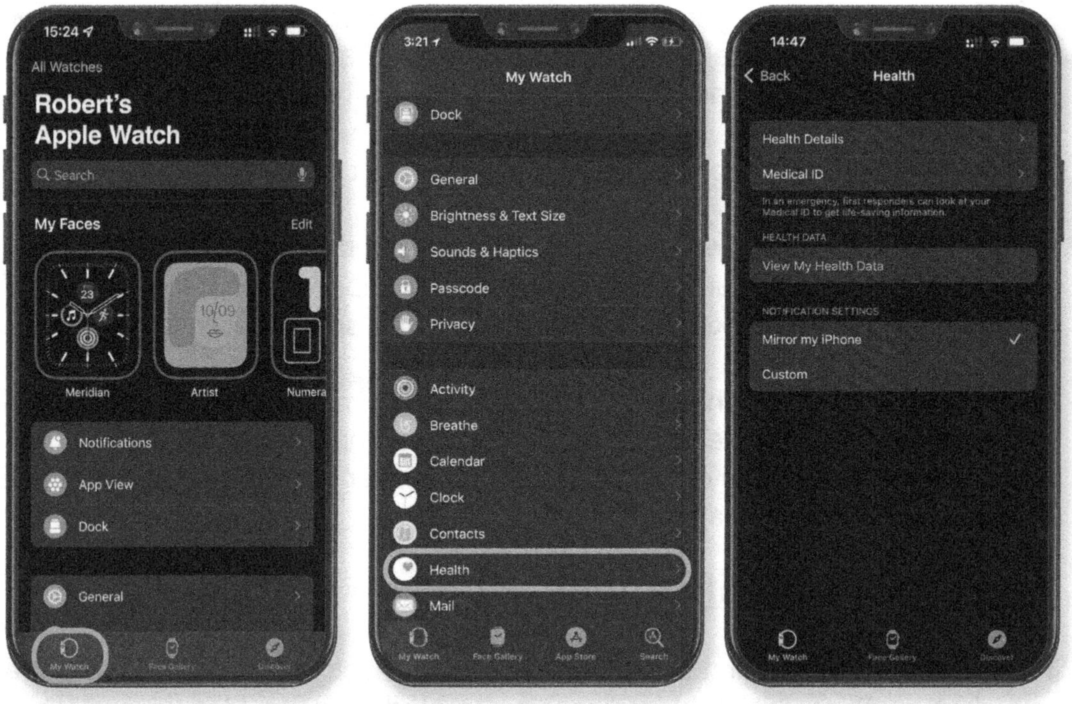

To **enable heart rate notifications** on your **Apple Watch**, open the **Watch app** on your **iPhone**. Tap the **My Watch tab** at the bottom of the screen and select **Heart** from the list. Here you can enable or disable Irregular Rhythm notifications and set the parameters for your high and low heart rate notifications by defining the beats per minute. For example, you may choose a value of 120 beats per minute, and your **Apple Watch** will notify you if your heart rate remains at or above this level for 10 minutes.

Along with these notifications, your Apple Watch can also assess your cardio fitness level by calculating how your heart reacts to different types of exercise. It does this by estimating your VO2 max, which measures how

much oxygen your body can use during training in mL/kg/min. A person with a very high VO2 max can sustain intense bouts of exercise for much longer than someone with a low VO2 max. Your **Apple Watch** will look at how fast you can recover after a workout while considering your age, sex, weight, and heights, to estimate your VO2 max and determine your cardio fitness level.

You can choose to enable notifications that will alert you when your cardio fitness drops below a certain level, hopefully encouraging you to partake in more regular exercise. You do not need to do strenuous exercise to stay healthy, and slow walks are just as good at keeping your heart healthy.

ECG App

One of the newer features introduced to the **Apple Watch** series is the ECG app, which can produce an electrocardiogram (ECG). This measures the strength and timing of the electrical signals that make up your heartbeat. ECGs are a great way to learn more about your heart rhythm, and doctors often use them to diagnose different conditions.

The ECG app uses the electrical heart sensor in the **Digital Crown** of your **Apple Watch** to record this data. The ECG app tests these electrical signals and compares them to your heartbeats to see if they are correctly timed.

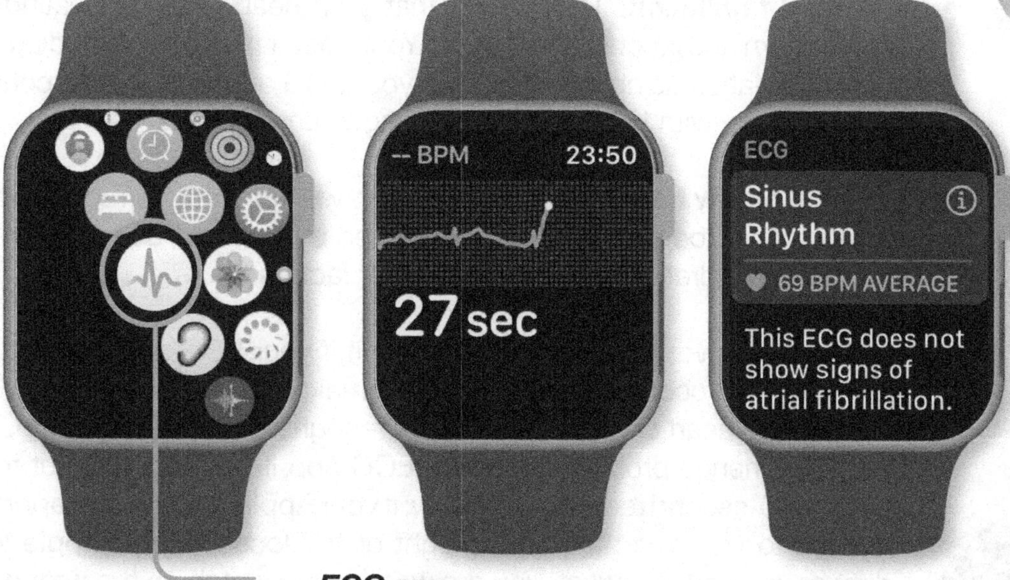

ECG app

You can set up the ECG app through the **Health app** on your **iPhone**. Select Heart from the list of health categories, tap Electrocardiograms (ECGs), and then tap Set up ECG App. You will need to fill in some information before taking your first ECG.

To take an ECG, open the **ECG app** on your **Apple Watch**. The app will ask you to rest your arm on a table or lap as you hold your index finger on the Digital Crown for 30 seconds. You will see a countdown during this time. Once completed, the app will review the data and determine if there are any irregularities in heart rhythm that may be of concern. You can see a graph showing the waveforms of your heartbeats and the electrical signals. You can also record any symptoms you may be experiencing to go along with your ECG. These results can be exported as a PDF and sent to your medical professional.

You can use the ECG app if you ever feel unusual heart symptoms such as chest pain or discomfort, nausea, indigestion, stomach pain or heartburn, or pain that starts in the chest and spreads to the left arm, feeling dizzy or lightheaded, unusual jaw or throat pain, feeling tired and weak, swelling, or an irregular heartbeat.

The **ECG app** can provide you with a limited number of results:

- **Sinus rhythm:** This is your heart rate and should fall between 50-100 beats per minute. A normal sinus rhythm does not necessarily mean that everything is working correctly, and there may still be problems worth talking to your doctor about.
- **Atrial fibrillation:** This means that your heart may be beating with an irregular pattern and inconsistent timing. Your doctor may be able to diagnose you with atrial fibrillation using the data from your ECG app after further consulations and provide you with treatment and management options.
- **High or low heart rate:** The ECG app will not work correctly if your heart rate is too high or too low. This may be caused by exercise, stress, nervousness, medications, dehydration, infections, or other factors.
- **Inconclusive:** You may see this result if your ECG app cannot generate a result. This may occur if you have a pacemaker, an implantable cardioverter-defribillator, or a heart condition that is not recognized by the ECG app.

You may experience problems with the ECG app if you move about too much during the 30-second recording window; if your **Apple Watch** is not appropriately secured to your wrist and is too tight or too loose; if your **Apple Watch** is dirty or covered by sweat, you are wearing the watch on the wrong wrist, or your orientation settings are not correct, or you are standing nearby other electronics that may cause interference. To get the best results, you will need

to follow the instructions carefully, make sure your watch is fitted securely, and is clean and dry.

Open the **Health app** on your **iPhone** to download and share your ECG results in PDF format. Tap Browse at the bottom of the display and then choose Heart. In the Heart section, tap Electrocardiograms (ECG) and then tap on the chart showing your most recent results. You will see a button that says: Export a PDF for Your Doctor. Press the Share button to print or share this document in an email or message.

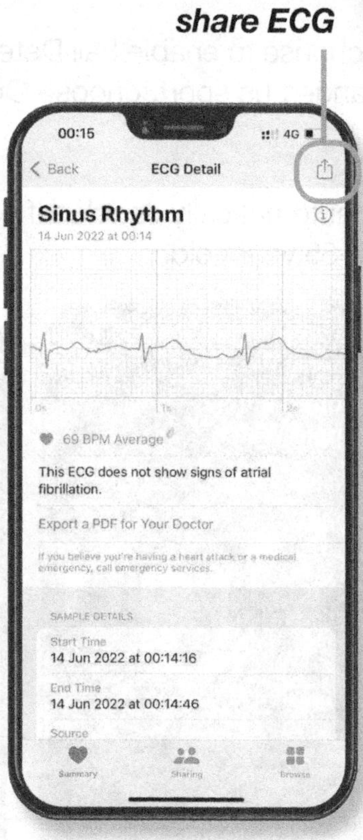

Fall Detection

Falling is one of the most common injuries experienced by seniors, and hundreds of thousands of people are hospitalized for fall-related injuries every year. A fall can easily lead to broken bones, brain injuries, or death.

Every year, more than 36 million older adults suffer from falls, leading to about 32,000 deaths. Approximately on ein every five of these falls leads to an injury, and more than 300,000 people require hospitalization for hip fractures from these falls (CDC, 2019).

Your **Apple Watch** can detect a fall using the internal accelerometer and gyroscope sensors. The sensors will be able to detect any hard impacts, even those from a car accident or a sporting injury. Though it may not be able to prevent these falls, it can help you get medical attention quickly and efficiently by contacting emergency services.

To turn on fall detection:

- Open the **Watch app** on your **iPhone**.
- Select **My Watch** from the tabs at the bottom.
- Scroll to and select **Emergency SOS.**

- Here, you can toggle **Fall Detection on or off.**

- You can choose to enable Fall Detection always, or if you participate in a high-impact or potentially dangerous sport, choose Only On During Workouts.

Fall Detection is automatically enabled if you enter your age into your **Apple Watch** upon setup and you are over 55 years old.

What happens when a fall is detected?

- When a hard impact is detected, your **Apple Watch** will alert you by sending taps to your wrist and sounding an alarm.

- You can see the alert on display, and you can choose to contact emergency services by swiping the SOS button to the right, or dismiss the alert by tapping I'm OK or the Close button in the upper left corner.

  - If the watch can detect that you are moving about, it will not immediately contact emergency services and will wait for your response.

  - However, if you are immobile for more than a minute, the alerts-tapping

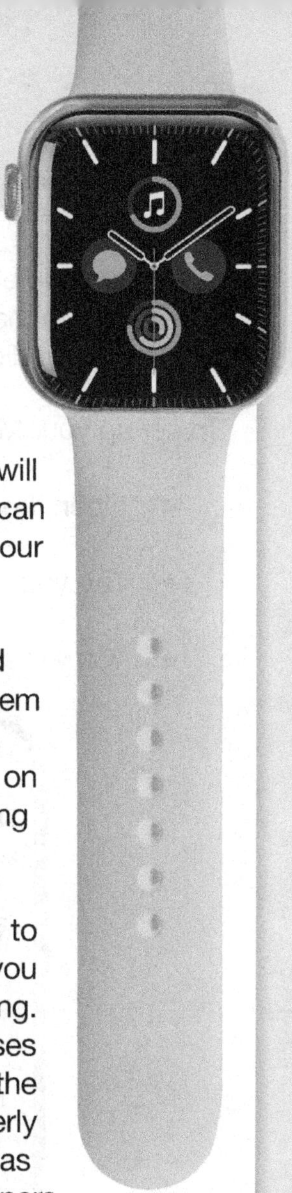

and sounds will become louder and more intense, with the goal of alerting someone nearby that you need assistance.

- If you are still unable to respond, your watch will automatically call emergency services for you. In the call, your **Apple Watch** will play an audio message explaining that it has detected a fall and you are unresponsive. It will provide the emergency services with details of your current location. You can also choose to share your medical ID so that emergency services can see your name, age, and other important medical information.

- When the call to emergency services is finished, your watch will send out an alert to your selected emergency contacts with a message to let them know that you have fallen and that medical services have been contacted.

You can view a history of your Fall Detection records through the Health app on your **iPhone.** You can find this information in the Other Data section by tapping on Number of Times Fallen.

Though Fall Detection is a great feature, you can also take some measures to help prevent falls in your own life. Make sure to let those around you know if you are on medications that may make you dizzy or increase your chances of falling. Make sure your vision is taken care of and that any prescriptions for glasses are up to date, and get checked for cataracts as you get older. Take care of the condition of your feet by seeing a podiatrist occasionally and wearing properly fitted shoes. If you are at risk of falling, try to make sure your home is as safe as possible by installing railings, removing trip hazards, and covering sharp corners or edges (CDC, 2019).

Emergency SOS

Another important feature that is related to Fall Detection but can be used in any situation is Emergency SOS. By enabling this feature, you can press and hold the side button on your **Apple Watch** to call emergency services without dialing a number or looking at your screen.

Medical ID and Emergency Contacts

It is essential to set up your Medical ID so that you can take advantage of all of the emergency features on your **iPhone** and **Apple Watch**. Your Medical ID contains critical information—your name, date of birth, medical conditions and other medical notes, allergies and reactions to medications you are on, blood type, organ donor information, weight, height, your primary language, and your emergency contact information—that emergency services can access without needing to unlock your devices. Suppose you ever find yourself in a situation where you need medical attention but cannot communicate effectively. In that case, your Medical ID can be used to answer all of the crucial questions that a paramedic, first responder, or doctor may need.

To set up your Medical ID:

- Open the **Health app** on your **iPhone**.
- Tap your profile picture at the top right of the screen.
- You will see **Health Details and Medical ID.**

- First, tap **Health Details**, and make sure all of the information is correct, including your first name, last name, date of birth, sex, an, if necessary, your blood type, Fitzpatrick skin type, whether or not you are wheelchair-bound or reliant, list any allergies of concern, and any medications that impact your heart rate.
- Next, go back and select **Medical ID.** If you are setting this up for the first time, you need to go through the list and fill in all the relevant information. Make sure to add your emergency contacts and assign them to the right relationship.

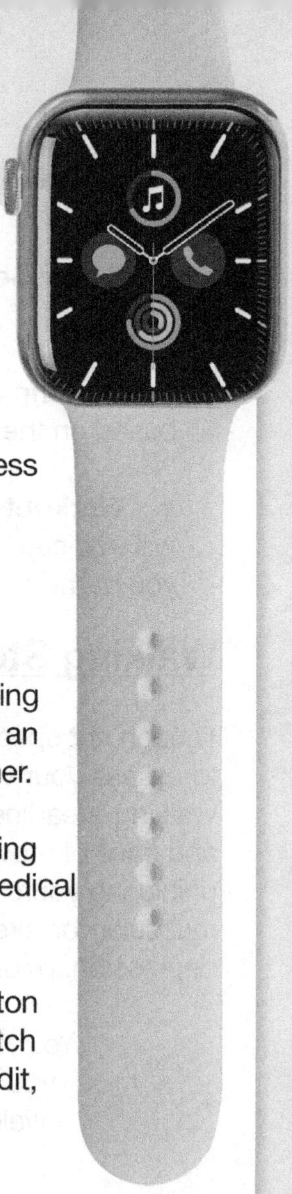

- If you have contacts saved with a nickname or something similar to 'mother,' 'daughter,' 'doctor,' consider changing their contact information to include their names to make it easier for any emergency services to communicate with them.

- At the bottom of the Medical ID settings, ensure that Emergency Access is set to Show When Locked.

- Tap Done in the top right corner when you are finished.

You can now see your Medical ID from the lock screen on your **iPhone** by swiping up and selecting Emergency from the lower-left corner. This will direct you to an emergency dialing screen where you can tap Medical ID in the lower-left corner.

You can also view your Medical ID on your **Apple Watch** by pressing and holding the side button until you see the menu appear. You will find the Power Off, Medical ID, and Emergency SOS sliders on this menu.

If, for some reason, you do not see your Medical ID when holding the side button on your **Apple Watch**, open the Watch app on your **iPhone**. Select My Watch from the bottom of the screen and then tap Health. Select Medical ID and Edit, then make sure the feature for Show When Locked is enabled.

Medical Trends

Using the **Health app** on your **iPhone**, you can easily find visual summaries of all your health and wellness data that has been collected on your **Apple Watch** and **iPhone** under the **Health Trends section.**

- **Steps:** See the daily average number of steps taken.

- **Active energy:** See how many calories you burn per day on average.

- **Flights climbed:** See how many flights of stairs you have climbed per day on average. This value is calculated based on how much elevation you gain each day as you go about your activities.

- **Resting heart rate:** See your average resting heart rate. The more data points your Health app has access to, the more accurate this will be, and you can see if your resting heart rate has decreased or increased over time.

- **Sleep:** See how many hours you are getting on average and compare this to your sleep goal.

- **Walking and running distance:** See how many miles or kilometers you cover per day, based on the number of steps you take and any running or walking workouts.

- **Workouts:** See how many hours you spend being active and working out each day. You will also see how many days you have worked out in the past month and how many calories you burned on average during these workouts.

Walking Steadiness

Though not specifically related to your **Apple Watch**, your iPhone health app can also be used to assess your walking steadiness, a helpful measure to determine if you are at risk of falling. Walking steadiness is your ability to control your movements, demonstrating good balance and ease of movement in different situations. This can decline as you age, leaving you at risk of injuring yourself through a fall. Walking steadiness can also be affected by neurological, muscular, or skeletal conditions ranging from stroke, previous injury, chronic pain, arthritis, depression, poor vision, inner ear problems, etc.

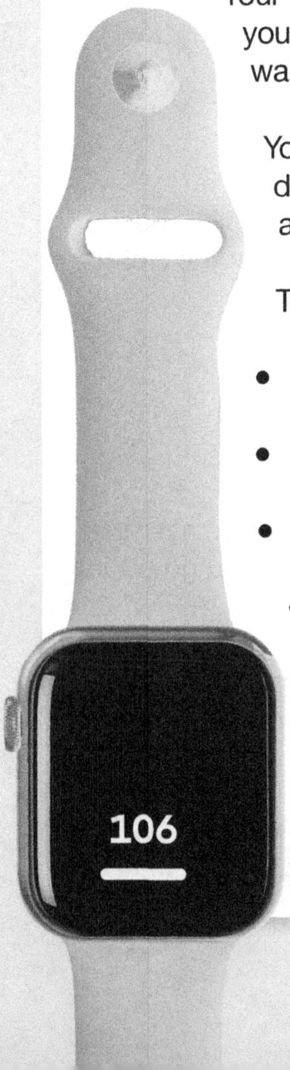

Your **iPhone** will measure your walking steadiness by assessing your gait—how you walk, including your walking speed, length of stride, double support time, and walking asymmetry. It will rate your walking steadiness as OK, Low, or Very Low.

You can use walking steadiness information to identify potential fall risks or declines in walking ability and balance. The app will suggest several exercises and mobility activities to help you improve your walking steadiness.

To set up Walking Steadiness:

- Open the **Health app** on your **iPhone.**
- Tap the **Summary button** at the bottom of the screen.
- Scroll down to the **Walking Steadiness** tab and select it.
- Press **Set Up.**
- You will need to follow some of the prompts and fill in your details, such as birth date, weight, and height.

- You must also read through some of the Walking Steadiness information and how the different levels are determined.

- Tap **Done** when you are finished.

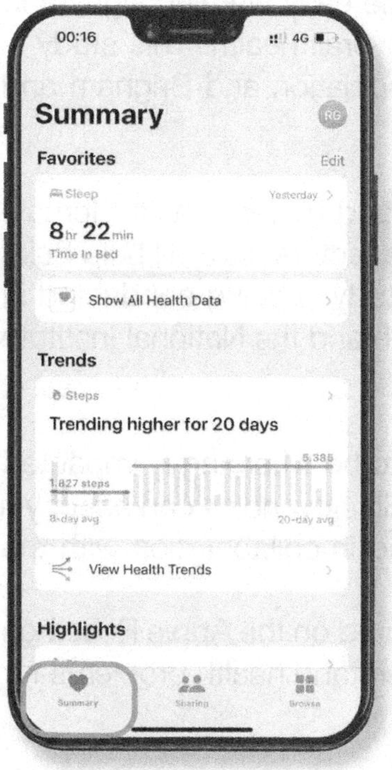

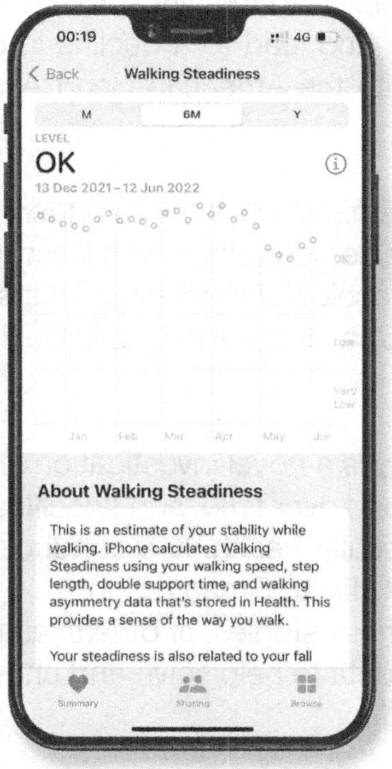

Your **iPhone** will only be able to collect data on walking steadiness if you have it on your person while walking and moving about.

Apple Research App

One of the final points to mention is the Apple Research App. Using your **iPhone** and **Apple Watch**, you can help contribute to health studies and research by sharing your health data. This significantly reduces the time and expense generally required to carry out extensive medical studies. It can help contribute to the development of new and novel technologies, treatments, and a general improvement in our understanding of different medical conditions and how they impact other people.

You can choose which studies you would like to participate in through the Medical Research app based on your eligibility. Each study will be unique, and some may ask you to fill in some information while others may only collect your health data. None of the studies will receive your personal information or contact details. Rest assured that just like in a typical medical study, your data will not be sold to any party. You get to decide which ones to participate in, and you can leave at any time. You can control which types of data you want to share, and the studies are obligated to provide you with feedback on exactly how your data will be used to support their research.

Some of the ongoing research includes

- **The Apple Heart and Movement Study:** This study looks into the relationship between heart health and physical activity, helping to identify some of the early warning signs and factors that can impact heart health and lead to a decline in overall health. This study is being conducted in collaboration with the American Heart Association and Brigham and Women's Hospital.

- **Apple Women's Health Study:** This study aims to understand better how the female reproductive cycles are impacted by demographics and lifestyle factors and will help build better screening procedures for gynecologic conditions. This study is being conducted in collaboration with the Harvard T. H. Chan School of Public Health and the National Institute of Environmental Health Sciences.

- **Apple Hearing Study:** This study is a novel investigation into how hearing is impacted by exposure to different levels of sound over time, and specifically how noise can affect your hearing, stress levels, and cardiovascular health. It is conducted in collaboration with the University of Michigan and the World Health Organization.

Your contributions to any of these studies, or others featured on the Apple Research app, can provide essential data to help solve and understand health problems for millions of people worldwide.

In Summary

By now, you can appreciate how much your **Apple Watch** can benefit you and your overall health. It can be a valuable way to assess how well you are progressing and improve your physical fitness while monitoring the condition of your heart and looking out for any red flags or warning signs. You will become more informed and have a better understanding of the patterns of your heart so that you can confidently identify any irregularities or areas of concern. You will also be able to assist your doctors and medical professionals in treating and diagnosing any heart conditions or symptoms you experience, leading to more efficient and tailored treatment optionsefficient and tailored treatment options.

Your **Apple Watch** also offers you methods of managing and dealing with stress through the Mindfulnes app. These calming benefits should not be forgotten or underappreciated, as needless stress and anxiety can take years off your life. Protect your hearing so that you never feel left out in conversations with your loved ones, and make sure you do not expose yourself to loud

noises that could cause damage. Stay on top of your hygiene practices and combat the spread of viruses and bacteria with the handwashing app. Finally, by setting up fall detection and your Apple ID, you can always contact emergency services and emergency contacts, even if you have taken a nasty fall and are unconscious.

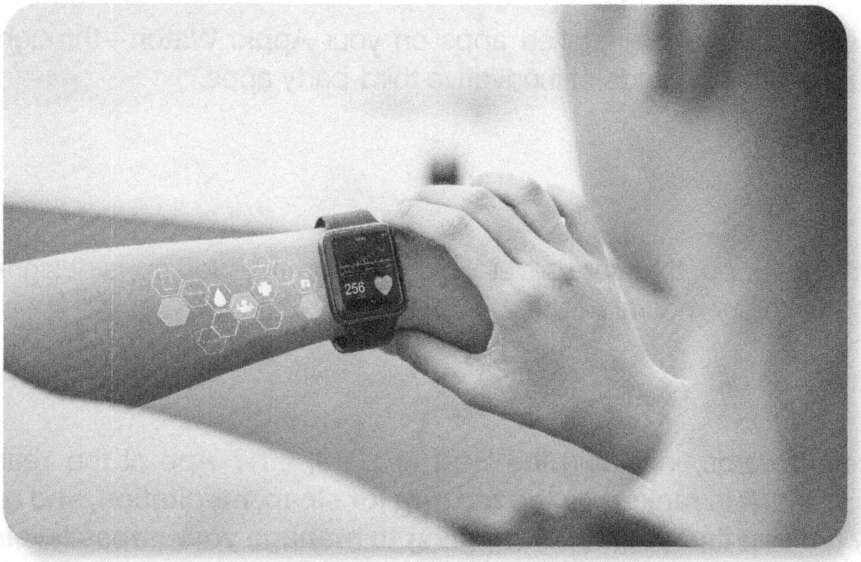

CHAPTER 5: Best Apps

You don't have to settle for the preinstalled apps on your **Apple Watch**—through the App Store, you can get access to hundreds of innovative third-party apps.

Mindfulness

Along with the Mindfulness app, there are several highly recommended apps designed to help you manage and improve your mental health.

Calm

Calm has won several awards, including the Best of 2018, 2017 App of the Year, and the Happiest App in the World. **It is ranked as the top app for sleep, meditation, and relaxation, and you should try it if you find yourself struggling to manage your stress levels or sleep patterns.**

The app provides you with guided meditations, breathing programs, stretching exercises, relaxing and calming music, and stories to help you sleep. You can access hundreds of different programs geared towards your specific needs, experience level, and available periods.

The guided meditations have different focuses, ranging from deep sleep to happiness and gratitude, self-esteem, relationships, calming anxiety, and mindful walking. The bedtime stories are narrated by some of the world's most beloved voices, including Stephen Fry and Matthew McConaughey.

Calm app

One of the most understated features is the soundscapes, which help to immerse you in ocean waves or near a campfire as you meditate.

Calm is a subscription-based service that offers a free trial period, and it can collect and save all your meditation data and sleep sessions directly into the Apple Health app. It integrates seamlessly with your **Apple Watch** to provide you with different sessions and monitor your health stats.

Headspace

Headspace is quite similar to the Calm app but stands out in how it works with the Apple Watch, offering you meditations and breathing exercises right on your wrist, whether or not you have it installed on your iPhone. The goal of the Headspace app is not only to help you with your mental health but also to equip you with tools and strategies so that you will always be able to deal with complicated feelings without relying on the app. Each day a new topic is selected as the focus, so you will never get bored with the meditations.

Headspace offers sleep and guided meditations, as well as a Move Mode, which you can use to help relieve tension in your body by following a series of very basic movements and intentions. One of the best features is the SOS meditation—short three-minute sessions to help you pull yourself together in no time-which is great for difficult situations with family or at work when you feel overwhelmed and need a helping hand. You can also take advantage of the focus-enhancing music that allows you to concentrate and be more productive. This is also a subscription-based service with a few payment options and a free trial period.

Sleep

AutoSleep

A sleek and intelligently designed app that builds upon the foundations of the Apple Sleep app to provide you with more significant insights into your sleep patterns. **AutoSleep is an automatic sleep-tracking app that will begin monitoring your sleep using the Apple Watch without the need to press any buttons.** You can adjust your AutoSleep settings to suit your needs so that the data will be more accurate—

tell the app if you are a light sleeper or a restless sleeper, help it figure out when you go to bed and when you wake up, and what kind of lifestyle you lead. You can see detailed reports after each night's sleep to help you develop better nighttime routines and alter your sleeping habits to improve the quality of your sleep.

Auto sleep uses the heart rate monitor on your **Apple Watch** to determine the quality of your sleep by looking at how much time you spent asleep while lying in bed, analyzing how restless you are, and how your heart rate changes during the night to develop a comprehensive sleep analysis report each morning. If you have a later model of the **Apple Watch**, you can even use AutoSleep to monitor your blood oxygen levels as you sleep, which can be used by people with sleep apnea and other conditions that affect breathing during the night.

You can add AutoSleep complications to your **Apple Watch** watch faces to see some of the most interesting and important pieces of information. One of the best features of AutoSleep is the Readiness rating, which is a simple estimate of your "daily readiness" that takes into account your physical and mental stress levels and the quality of your sleep. Sleep readiness is determined using many different data points from your Health app, including your heart rate, exercise data, and sleep data.

AutoSleep has smart alarms that you can set that help you wake up without being startled by your usual alarm's harsh beeping or annoying sounds. These smart alarms work over a few minutes and take advantage of the haptic vibrations in the **Apple Watch** to 'tickle' or 'nudge' you every few minutes, just before you are set to wake up. The smart alarm will determine if you are in a deep sleep or light sleep phase and decide which method will best wake you up.

AutoSleep includes a charge reminder so that you can charge your watch a few minutes before your bedtime, ensuring the battery will last throughout the night. You can also set Day Time or Night Time watch faces that display all the relevant data fields, and you can easily switch between these just like any other **Apple Watch** faces.

Sleep Cycle

This is another highly-rated sleep app that integrates with your Apple Watch. Analyze the quality of your sleep by using the accelerometers and gyroscopes in your **Apple Watch** to see how restless you are during the night and generate detailed reports about your breathing rate as you sleep. It features smart alarms, where you can set wake windows. For example, if you set the alarm for 6:00 am with a 30-minute sleep window starting at 5:30 am, the app will wait until it detects you are entering a light sleep phase before it will

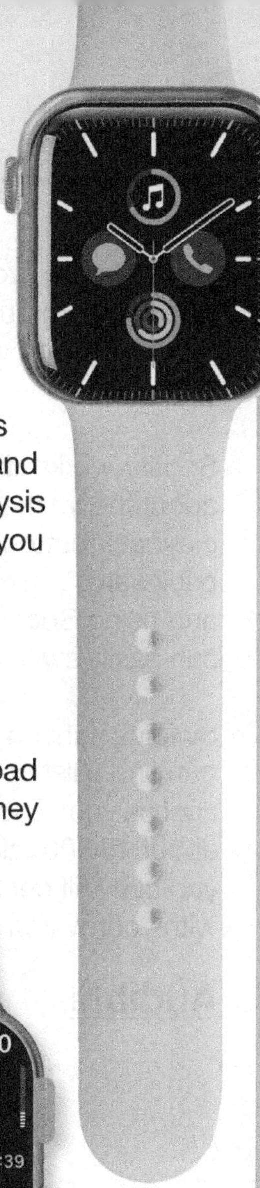

begin to wake you. This helps prevent you from waking up during deep or REM sleep, which can be stressful or frustrating, and helps you have a more peaceful and productive day.

Sleep Cycle also offers an extensive library of music, meditations, and stories that have been carefully curated to help promote sleep by reducing anxiety and stress and allowing you to relax. Each morning you can access your sleep analysis record, and the app can help correlate external and lifestyle factors to help you figure out what may be impacting your sleep quality.

Media

You are not limited to Apple Music on your **Apple Watch**. You can also download other media apps that give you access to exclusive content and value-for-money payment plans.

Spotify

You have likely heard of Spotify if you are not already using it.

It is one of the world's most extensive music streaming services, providing you with music on-demand directly to your devices.

Spotify can be downloaded for almost any device, including your **iPhone, Apple Watch,** iPad, laptop, desktop, and even your TV or PlayStation.

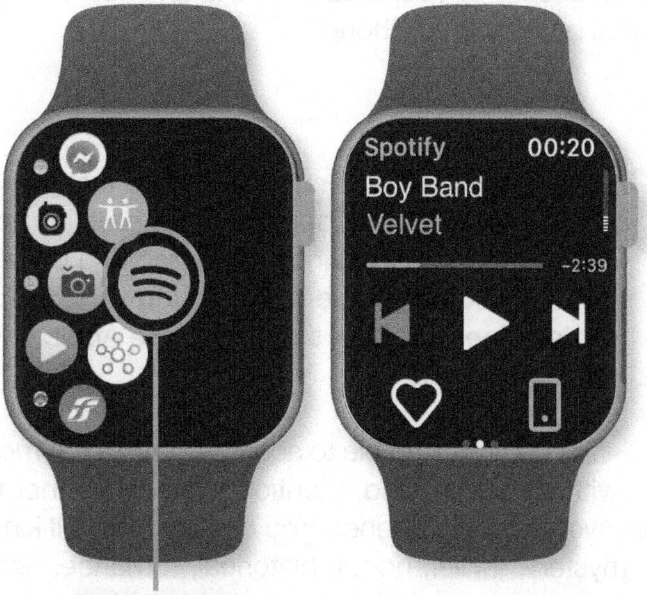

Spotify app

Though Spotify is a subscription-based service, you can also use it for free, though some of the features will be limited, and you will occasionally have to listen to ads.

Spotify gives you access to millions of songs from any artist or album you can think of. You can also listen to podcasts and take advantage of the carefully curated charts to see what is trending and popular and find new genres to peak your interest.

Using Spotify, you can also find playlists, compiled by the Spotify team and members of the listening community, to suit any mood or activity. Find playlists for a lazy Sunday afternoon, a long drive filled with nostalgia, or something more upbeat while you finish some work around the house.

Spotify works directly through your **Apple Watch**, where you can see important information about the track you are listening to, such as the title, artist, and remaining time left. The control playback buttons are simple and easy to use, allowing you to pause, play, or skip forward or backward. You can also add or remove tracks to your favorites simply by tapping the heart icon and using Spotify connect to play the audio out of your nearby Bluetooth devices, which you can easily switch between.

Swiping right on your Spotify main screen will take you to the Recently Played menu, where you can find a list of all the tracks and podcasts you have listened to most recently. You can also access your Spotify Library and Downloads here. Using your **Apple Watch**, you can download about 10,000 minutes of listening material, so that even if you don't have your **iPhone** nearby, you can still get access to your music. This is an excellent feature if you want to go for a walk with your watch but not your **iPhone**.

Audible

More and more people struggle to find the time or patience to sit down and read books; however, audiobooks are the perfect replacement that allows you to reap all the benefits of reading while still doing other tasks. With **Audible, you can listen to some of the best-selling audiobooks and podcasts to keep you entertained for hours on end.** Use Audible when traveling, cleaning, walking, or just relaxing.

You can use Audible to access some of the most famous literary works, narrated with great care and attention to detail so that the true essence is captured and conveyed to the listener. You can also find all kinds of genres, ranging from crime, mystery, thriller, horror, historical, romance, and western, as well as many non-fiction categories like history, biographies, memoirs, travel, philosophy, religion, and spirituality, self-help, finance, science, and more.

Audible offers you subscription options that give you a free credit each month that you can spend on any title in their library while also providing massive discounts of up to 80% off premium titles.

Use the Audible app on your **Apple Watch** by downloading it onto your **iPhone** and then syncing your library. You can choose which titles to sync to

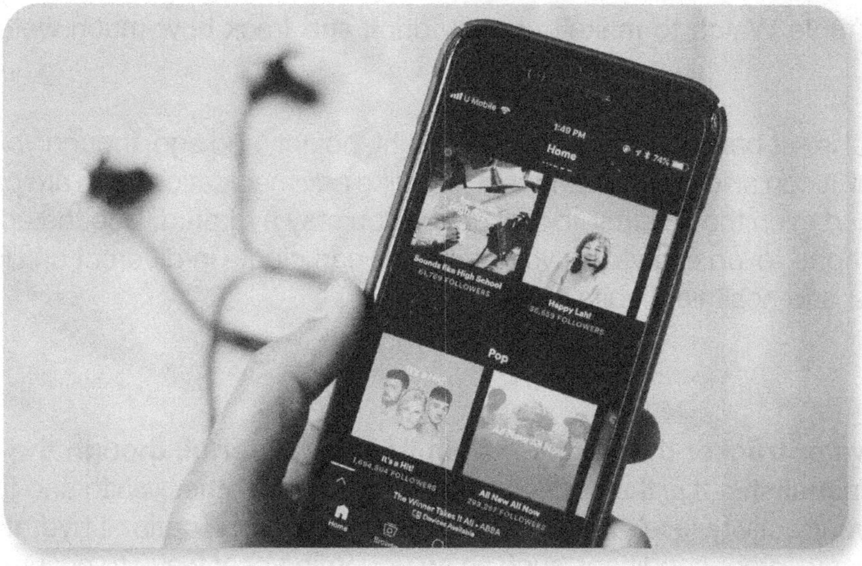

your **Apple Watch**, helping you save on storage space. Listen to your audiobooks using a Bluetooth device like headphones or a speaker.

The **Apple Watch** app lets you control the playback and gives you the option of skipping forward or backward 30 seconds, so you never miss anything important. One of the best features is the sleep timer, which you can access by tapping the small clock icon. With this feature, you can set the desired time, after which the playback will stop. Many people find audiobooks so relaxing that they use them to fall asleep, which ensures that the playback doesn't continue right through the night, causing you to miss out on all the action. You can also speed up or slow down the pace of the narration.

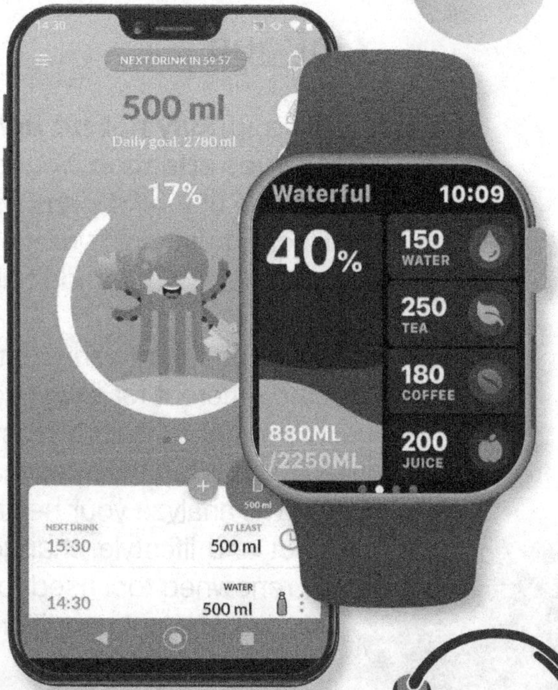

Health Apps

Keep an eye on your water intake to make sure you are always hydrated with these fun apps that can provide some interesting insights:

Waterful

This cute and quirky app features a purple octopus who acts as your hydration coach to help you drink enough water every day. The app sends you reminders to your **Apple Watch** to make sure you drink and track how much water you get through each day.

Your daily water goal is set based on your gender, weight, height, and age, though you can also customize your goal. It can also consider other factors like any medications you are prescribed, your activity level, and even the weather to make sure you stay hydrated. Use the app on your watch or on your **iPhone** to log everything you drink and participate in different challenges that help you build better and healthier habits.

Thirsty

Thirst is a smart water tracker that functions similarly to Waterful, though the design is more sleek and minimalistic. It is the perfect companion to your other health and fitness apps that can adapt to your activity level and lifestyle to determine your optimal hydration goals. The app can consider weather conditions such as an upcoming heat wave to ensure you drink enough water and can fend off any chance of heatstroke.

Thirst will send you notifications to help remind you to drink water, and you can easily record your daily water intake by logging your drinks. The app aims to get you to drink a lot of small amounts several times throughout the day, rather than simply trying to hit a goal at the end of the day. It can integrate with your Health app to provide a more comprehensive analysis of your hydration needs and help you achieve them to always feel your best.

GoPoop

This app may not be right for everybody, but your digestive system also deserves attention. Your digestion can tell you a lot about your health, and it is often one of the firt signs that something may be wrong. With all of the focus on fitness, nutrition, hydration, sleep, and heart health, why not spend some time understanding your poop habits better?

With GoPoop, you can create a logbook every time you visit the bathroom, and record different features like regularity, shape, color, constipation, etc. You can use your **Apple Watch** to swipe through the other characteristics, and all you need to do is tap the ones that best describe your poop. With this information, the app will analyze your health and advise you to improve your digestion through diet and lifestyle changes. The app uses the Bristol Stool Scale, a world-renowned tool used to analyze poops and figure out how to treat different bowel and gut conditions.

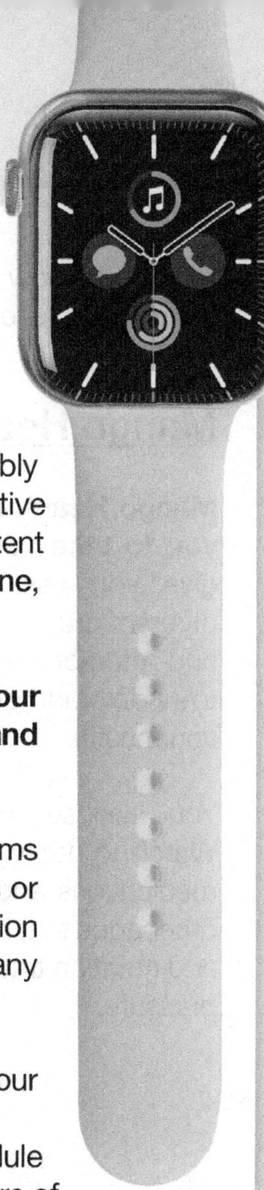

The app is entirely free, and you can install a companion app on your **Apple Watch** so you can log your poops at any time.

WebMD: Symptom Checker

If you have ever looked up your medical symptoms online, you were probably directed to one of WebMD's thousands of well-researched and informative articles. They are one of the largest online human health and wellness content publishers. There is also a WebMD app that you can download onto your **iPhone**, with some convenient features you can set up on your **Apple Watch**.

The WebMD Symptom Checker app is the place to check any of your symptoms, create reminders for your medications, view allergy alerts, and receive the latest news and updates on health-related topics.

The symptom checker feature allows you to input any number of symptoms you may be experiencing, and the app will suggest any possible conditions or issues that may be related. From there, you can read the thorough information to determine whether or not you may need to visit a doctor or if there are any treatment plans you could try at home first.

With the medication reminders, you can input all of the information about your medications, dosages, precautions, and side effects and receive reminders whenever it is time to take them. You can see your daily medication schedule with any important instructions to keep in mind, and you can also see a picture of the pills so that you never get them mixed up. You can sync your reminders straight to your **Apple Watch** to view them at any time.

To set up medication reminders, you will need to use the app on your **iPhone**, where you can select your medications from a list and choose an image from a preset list to accompany them. You can also add custom medications and add your own pictures if you cannot find the correct information from the provided list. Next, select what time you need to be reminded to take the medication. These notification will now be sent to your wrist, where you can snooze or dismiss the reminders. You can view the reminders by glancing at your **Apple Watch**, where you will see your upcoming doses and the scheduled time for taking them. When the next dose is due in two hours, you will see a count-down timer instead of the scheduled time. You can also mark doses as taken, missed, or skipped, and the app will keep a detailed record that you can refer back to at any time.

The allergy tracker is a helpful feature for keeping track of pollen counts in the air, dust, pollution, mold spores, and other allergy forecasts. You can set your location to view the levels in your area and get alerts when levels in your area are particularly high.

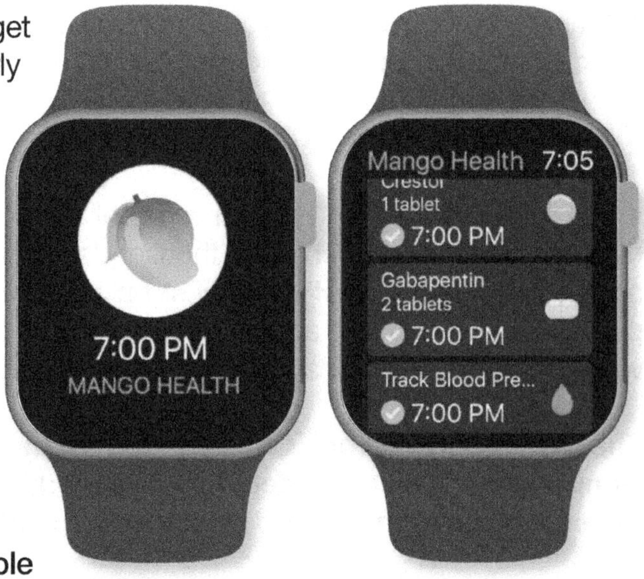

Mango Health

Mango Health is an app that reminds you to take your medication and can give you essential information about different drugs, including their effects and interactions. The app has an easy-to-understand design that helps to simplify your health.

You can set up reminders on your **Apple Watch** to notify you when it is time to take your medications and supplements. Several other reminders combine the features seen in some other apps that have been mentioned, such as reminders to drink water, a mood tracker, a food and nutrition tracker, a step counter, and alerts for checking your blood glucose levels or blood pressure.

You can easily find important information about all the drugs you are prescribed in the app, which will alert you to any side effects and interactions with other medications, foods, or supplements. The warnings are all color-coded to know which ones are more important. If you stick to your schedule without missing any doses, the app will reward you with points. As you collect more points, you stand a chance to win exclusive rewards such as gift cards or charity donations, though this is only available in selected regions. Mango Health can also help you manage your doctor's appointments and make sure you get your next prescription before you run out of medication.

Overall, Mango Health is a great app to make your medication regime a little more fun, with a design that is easy to look at and intuitive reminders to keep you on top of things.

ElderCheck Now

This minimalistic app is designed to let those who care about you know how you are doing at the touch of a button. It is more of a check-in app than a communication platform. Through Eldercheck Now, your caregivers can request a check-in from you. You can quickly respond to the request by

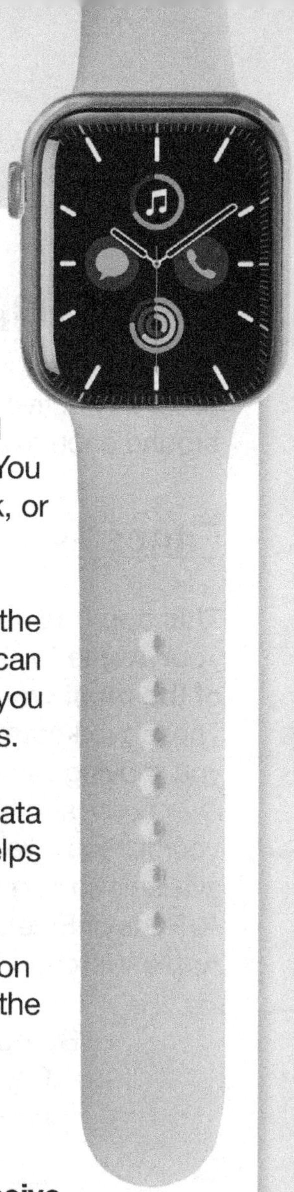

selecting 'I'm OK' or 'Call me!' directly on your **Apple Watch** or your **iPhone**. You can add pictures of your caregiver into the app so their face will come up any time you receive an alert.

ElderCheck lets you schedule check-ins to ensure everybody is safe and healthy before bed, while out on a walk, or after a doctor's appointment. You can schedule check-ins at any time of day and repeat them every day, week, or month.

When responding to a check-in request, your caregiver will be able to see the time that you responded and your location. This is a good safety feature that can alert your caregivers if something has gone wrong and you cannot answer. If you do not respond to a check-in request, the app will continue to send you alerts.

One of the best features of this app is that it can share your heart rate data with your caregivers every time you respond to their check-in request. This helps them monitor your health even if they cannot be by your side.

To get all of the benefitst out of ElderCheck you must have the app installed on your phone and your caregiver's phone, and also make sure to enable all the permissions such as health and location data.

Emergency: Alerts

This app is developed by the American Red Cross Society to help you receive accurate information and alerts about climate-related hazards. Just set your location, and the locations of your loved ones, and the app will alert you whenever there is a risk of severe weather, such as tornadoes, hurricanes, floods, fires, etc. The app lets you enable alerts and push notifications that you can tap to see more information. You can set the alerts to override Do Not Disturb mode so that you can be notified of an emergency even if you are asleep or busy with other tasks. There are 4 different customizable alerts that you can enable or disable, and customize the notifications to suit your particular needs.

The app will direct you to the nearest Red Cross shelter if you need to find a safe place during the weather event, and you can also see an interactive map with detailed overlays such as radar, satellite, clouds, rain, wind speed, and snowfall. You can also receive step-by-step guides that will help you prepare and stay safe during a disaster if you cannot get to a shelter.

Fitness Apps

Many fitness apps are available, and each is developed to suit a specific need. Whether you are pretty active and visit the gym to use their cardio machines and weights or struggle to move around enough during the day, you can find an app to help you get healthier.

Fitness+

This app has a built-in feature that comes with your Apple Watch, giving you access to some of the most welcoming and inclusive workouts. These workouts help you build better habits, get you moving more often, build confidence in your own body, and try something new, no matter what your fitness level is. It is a subscription service only available in some countries and works best with AirPods or Bluetooth headphones paired with your **Apple Watch**.

By opening your Fitness app on your **iPhone**, you can find **Fitness+** at the bottom of the screen.

This will take you to a browse page where you can search for and select workouts. Searching for older adult workouts will lead you to a workout series by Apple trainer Molly Fox, where you can partake in video-guided exercises that last only about 10 minutes. These workouts improve your strength, flexibility, mobility, balance, and coordination. You don't even need any special equipment, just your own body and a chair or wall to help with balance. The app can suggest any modifications if you struggle with a particular movement and includes only low-impact activities with minimal risk of causing injury.

Through Fitness+, you can also find more advanced or specialized workouts, like yoga or Pilates, strength training, and high-intensity interval training.

Try out the Time to Walk, an exclusive feature that comes with Fitness+. You can listen to some of your favorite public speakers as they tell you engaging and motivating stories to accompany you while you walk. You can get access to several episodes, each featuring a new guest who will discuss their

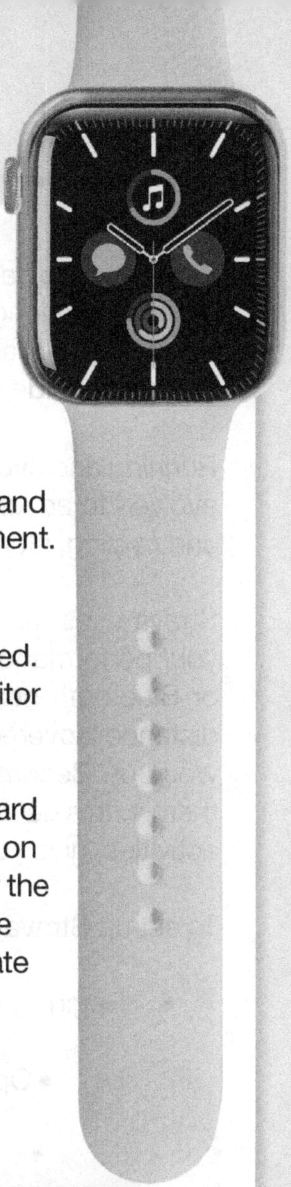

personal life, important moments, life lessons, touching memories, thoughts on purpose and gratitude, and other inspiring topics. As the guests talk, their stories will be narrated by photos you can view on your **Apple Watch**. Some of the most notable guests include Jane Fonda, Dolly Parton, Shawn Mendez, and more.

You can change from Time to Walk to Time to Push if you are in a wheelchair, and the exercises will be modified so that you can still reap the benefits of movement.

Your health stats will be recorded in the fitness app so you can review your progress and see how many steps you took or how many calories were burned. Of course, you can also see all of your heart rate data so that you can monitor your heart health.

To subscribe to Fitness+ you will need to make sure you have the standard Fitness app downloaded onto your **iPhone**. You can also use the version on your iPad or Apple TV. In the Fitness app, you will find a Fintess+ button near the bottom of the screen. Here, you can select a free trial option where you will be asked to fill in and confirm your Apple ID details. Follow the prompts to activate your subscription and reap all of the benefits.

Strava

Strava is one of the most popular fitness apps, becoming famous for its excellent use of GPS tracking data. With Strava, you can map your run, walk, or cycle to see your routes and get all your workout data like distance, pace, speed, elevation, and calories burned. With Strava, you can see these stats at different points along your route—see zones where you walked faster or places where a hill slowed you down, and work to continuously improve and push yourself on the same path to bring down your time.

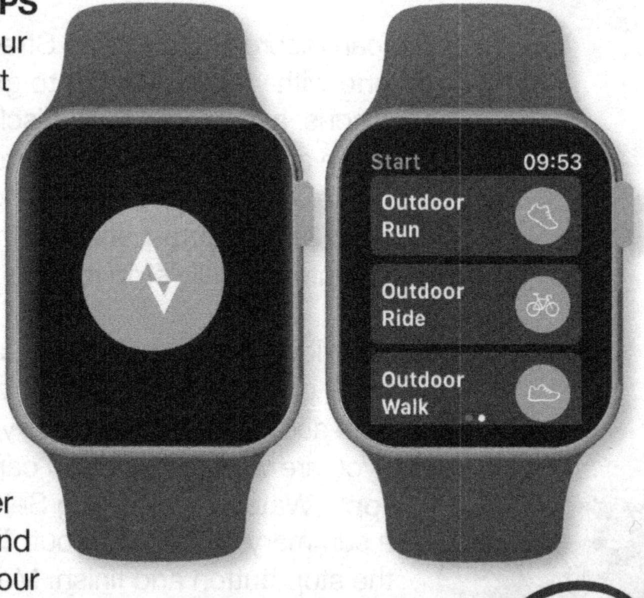

Through the Strava community, you can find new and exciting routes in your area that other people use. Get access to all kinds of maps and trails that you can try and contribute to with your own.

You can also take part in challenges and competitions through the Strava app. There are monthly challenges where you can hit specific goals and get rewarded. Enter competitions based on your age group, fitness level, and region so that you can have fun while pushing your limits alongside those at a similar level.

Running and cycling are the primary sports that made Strava the app it is today. However, it has evolved to accommodate many sports, including outdoor running and cycling, indoor running and cycling, standard gym workouts, walking, hiking, swimming, and many more.

Strava uses the heart rate data on your **Apple Watch** to monitor your heart rate and assess your performance. You can also receive audio cues through your **Apple Watch** to your Airpods or Bluetooth headset, giving you updates about your walk, hike, run, or cycle, such as the distance covered, current and average pace, and reminders to start, stop, or pause your workout. Become a part of the Strava community by sharing your workouts. You can share them with selected friends or a specific club or community. Your friends can comment on your activities, give you tips, and congratulate you on your achievements.

To set up Strava on your **Apple Watch**:

- Begin by downloading the **Strava app** onto your **iPhone** through the **app store.**
- Open the **Watch app** on your **iPhone** and select **My Watch.**
- Locate the Strava app and tap to install it on your **Apple Watch**.

You can record activity using Strava on your **Apple Watch** without carrying your **iPhone** with you. Make sure to give the app access to your location and health permissons, accept, the legal disclaimer, and turn on notifications when you first open the app on your **Apple Watch**. Then choose which sport type you want to do and select your preferred unit of measure: miles or kilometers. You can also choose to enable auto-pause so that if you take a break during your activity, the app will automatically stop recording.

You can view your elapsed time, average pace, split times, total distance, and heart rate on your **Apple Watch** during a workout. You will be able to turn on real-time audio feedback so that your watch will read this information out to you while you are working out. You can find these settings in the Strava app on your **Apple Watch** by selecting Settings and Audio Cues. You will be able to see a summary of your workout. To finish a workout, all you need to do is press the stop button and finish. Make sure you then choose to Save your activity so that it can be uploaded to your iPHone

Strava offers a complication that you can add directly to your watch face. This complication is just a shortcut that will take you directly to the app.

Outdooractive

This app is a great fit for you if you love hiking and walking in nature. It is much like most other types of fitness tracking apps—it can record and display your activity duration, route, ascent, descent, elevation, position, heart rate, and calories burned.

However, Outdooractive is unique because it uses GPS to help you navigate on trails using audio cues so that you can safely explore the wilderness without fear of getting lost or taking a wrong turn. The app helps to direct you by vibrating as you approach turns and when you go off-route. You can also see a direction arrow on your watch that points in the direction you need to travel. The arrow will point 50 meters ahead of you so that you can identify turns before you get to them.

You can use Outdooractive without your **iPhone**, which makes it a great choice for all-weather activities where your **iPhone** may be damaged by water, dust, and dirt. Unfortunately, the navigation features will be limited if your watch is not connected to your **iPhone**. You are able to download maps to your **Apple Watch** beforehand to get access to some of the best features while not connected to your **iPhone**. You will be able to see a map with your location on your watch, and you can easily pan or zoom in and out to see different locations. Switch between different map modes to see different aspects of the environment, like topography, satellite imagery, or standard view.

Hole19

This apps is a must-have for any avid golfer. Hole19 offers you a simple and easy way to keep score during your games. There are free andpaid versions of the app, but this one is definitely worth the price.

With the free version, you can access more than 43,000 different golf coursee with a map and GPS data of all the holes, hazards, greens, and other points of interest. Download the course you will be visiting to get all the information you will need to beat your score. You can even get accurate distance measurements from the front, back, and center of the greens. The app lets you create a digital scorecard to keep track of every stroke you take. You can see GPS distances on every golf course through your **Apple Watch** and create live leaderboards so that you can compete with your friends and compare your stats as you play.

The paid version comes with all of these features and more. You can access the helpful handicap calculator or challenge your friends to a match. The shot tracker feature is one of the most appealing—it gets precise measurements of your shots by measuring your starting and finishing postition, and records the data based on which club you used. The paid version can auto-detect when you move on to the next hole and provide a detailed report of your overall performance statistics and highlights. You can also access the full scoring capabilities through your **Apple Watch** and compare your game to the club statistics.

Utilities

Just Press Record

This is one of the most accessible audio recording apps you can find. With just one tap, you can record and capture important notes, spontaneous ideas, or special moments. This is not just a recording app, though, as it can take your audio files and transcribe them into text.

Just Press Record's recording feature is straightforward and easy to use. You can add the app to your **Apple Watch** and access it to start, stop, pause, or resume with just one touch.

Record on your **Apple Watch** and sync it with your **iPhone** at a later time. There is unlimited recording time, so you don't have to be rushed. You can also choose which audio input device to use: your **iPhone** microphone, the built-in **Apple Watch** microphone, AirPods, a Bluetooth headset, or even an external microphone. The app offers a lock screen widget, so you don't even

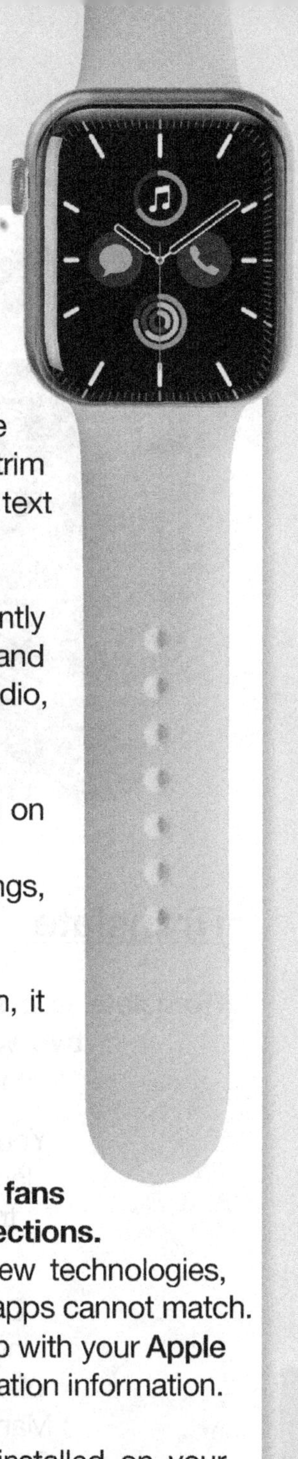

need to enter your passcode or unlock it to begin recording.

You can easily hear a playback of your audio recordings, and you can use the buttons to skip forward and backward, and adjust the speed. One of the best parts of this app is that it allows you to edit both the audio clips and the text transcripts. You can view a waveform of your audio clips where you can trim and cut out parts you don't need and make corrections or additions to your text transcripts.

The transcribe feature supports over 30 languages that you can set independently of your **Apple Watch** or **iPhone**'s settings. The app has punctuation command recognition, so you can speak the punctuation out loud as you record your audio, and it will be inserted into the text transcript.

Once you have your audio recordings and transcripts, you can share them on many different platforms through the app on your iPhone. There are several organization options, and you can browse through your library or recordings, renaming and sorting them as you need.

This is a highly underrated app, and though it may serve a simple function, it does so with excellence.

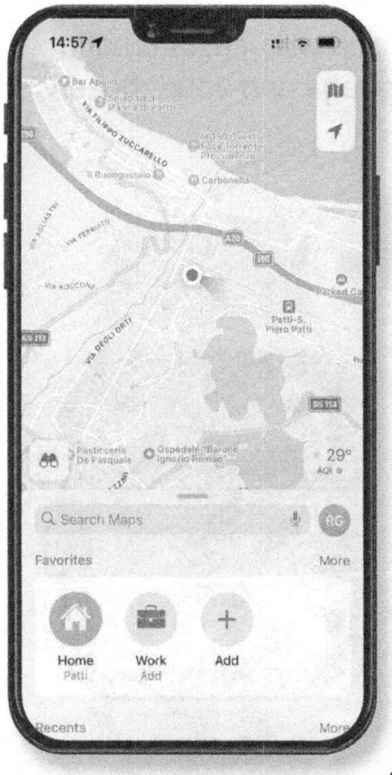

Google Maps

Even some of the most dedicated Apple fans often use Google Maps for navigating and directions. Thanks to its massive database and Street View technologies, Google Maps offeres several features that other apps cannot match. Luckily, you can integrate your Google Maps app with your **Apple Watch** to receive turn-by-turn directions and location information.

Make sure you have the **Google Maps app** installed on your **iPhone** and that you have saved essential locations like Work and Home. On your **Apple Watch**, you will see all of the places you have saved and begin navigating to them. Google Maps can give you turn-by-turn directions with audio alerts and help you find the fastest routes no matter what mode of transport you use, whether you walk, ride a bike, drive, or use public transit systems.

Now open the Google Maps app on your watch. You should see the shortcuts you created for home, work,

and other spots. Tap one of those shortcuts to receive turn-by-turn directions. At the same time, your phone will display a map and route to your destination.

You can tap the Start button in Google Maps on your **iPhone** to see directions on your phone and your watch.

iTranslate

iTranslate is a speech translation app that turns your Apple Watch or iPhone into a two-way translation device. With the iTranslate app, you can understand people speaking in different languages and even converse directly.

You can choose from 38 different languages, and the app will use automatic language detection to differentiate between your language and your chosen translation language.

Compatible languages include variations of: Arabic, Catalan, Mandarin, Taiwanese, Cantonese, Czech, Danish, Dutch, and different dialects of English, Finnish, French, German, Greek, Hebrew, Hindi, Hungarian, Indonesian, Italian, Japanese, Korean, Norwegian, Polish,

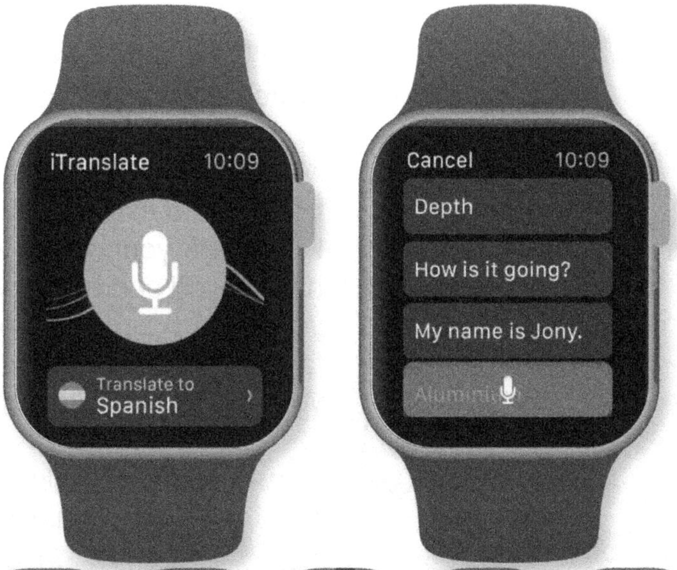

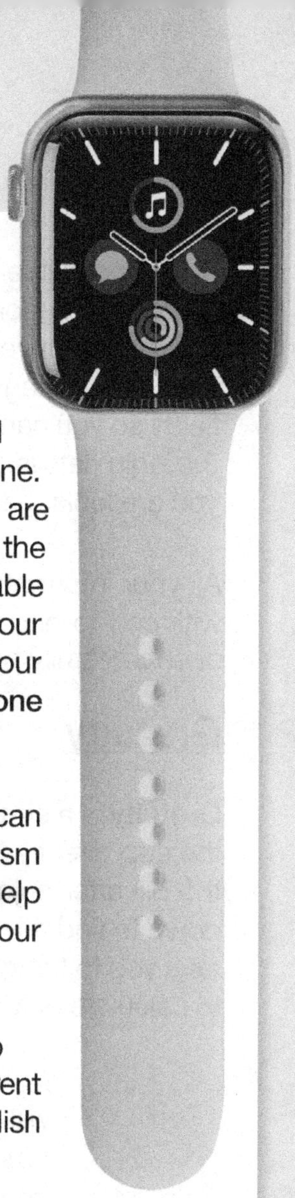

Portuguese, Romanian, Russian, Slovak, Spanish, Swedish, Thai, and Turkish.

The app is straightforward to use and has only a few buttons. Begin by selecting your language and the one you need to translate into. Then tap and hold the button on your **Apple Watch** display while speaking into the microphone. The app will automatically detect which of the two selected languages you are using and translate it to the other. It will use your **Apple Watch** speaker to play the translation spoken aloud. The person you are communicating with will be able to listen to and respond directly using the app in the same way, allowing your conversation to flow smoothly with minimal interruptions. You can also see your speech and the translated version in the text on your **Apple Watch** or **iPhone** display.

The speech detection in iTranslate works very well in most environments and can handle a lot of background noise, making it useful for travel and other tourism situations. It delivers your translations incredibly fast, in near real-time, to help your conversations feel more natural. You can also save transcripts of your conversations in text format to review them later.

iTranslate offers a complication to add to your watch face that you can tap to begin translating instantly. It will set a default language based on your current location; for example, if you travel to Mexico, the app can translate from English to Mexican Spanish.

You can also add a complication called Time Travel, which works by turning the **Digital Crown**. When you turn the **Digital Crown**, you will be able to see the phrases you have translated recently. This is a handy way to remember essential phrases for specific situations that may come up often.

1Password

Tired of being locked out of your devices or having to remember the passwords, passcodes, and other login information for all of your accounts? **With the 1Password app, you can safely and securely store all your important login information in one place, so that even if you do forget something, you can easily find it. With 1Password, all of your sensitive information is stored behind a single password, and this is the only one you will need to remember.**

1Password allows you to store any sensitive information you can imagine, from your **iPhone**'s password to your credit card details. The app also offers a password generator that you can use to create strong, unique, and unhackable passwords or memorizable pass-phrases for all of your online accounts. Organize your details into different categories so that they are easy to find: logines, credit card and bank details, addresses, driver's licenses, passports, social security, medical insurance, notes, and more. You can add tags or mark items as favorites to make them easier to find, and there are custom fields so you can add any extra information like a website URL or special note to go along with the login details. The app works with Spotlight search, so you can easily type in the information you are looking for into your search bar or use Siri to find it on your **Apple Watch**.

All your information will be protected by a single Master Password and everything is secured with end-to-end encryption. You can also access the app with your Face ID. You can also store or share family passwords for accounts like Netflix or Hulu through 1Password.

Gratuity

Gratuity is a simple calculator app designed to help you pay bills at restaurants. Download the app directly to your **Apple Watch** so you can access it from your wrist. When you receive the bill after enjoying your meal, you can open the app and use the **Digital Crown** to scroll down to find the total of your bill, no matter how large or small. Tap the value and the app will take you to the gratuity calculator where you can adjust the tip amount. The app makes it easy to calculate different tip values.

You can also choose to split the bill amongst your friends and family, and the app will easily calculate your total along with everybody else's and add in the gratuity amount for each person. Your preferred tipping amount will be remembered for the future, so you do not need to select it unless you choose a different tip in the future. The currency is automatically set based on your current location, but you can easily change this by accessing the settings.

Fit Brains Trainer

While there are dozens of apps to choose from that focus on improving your physical fitness, there are few that help you keep your mind sharp and healthy. **Fit Brains Trainer is an educational app that helps to stimulate your IQ and EQ** (cognitive and emotional intelligence) **to help prevent cognitive decline as we get older.** The app features mini-games, puzzles, and brain workout sessions and can generate in-depth reports for you to monitor your mental status. Fit Brains Trainer targets the six major areas of brain function: memory, speed of thinking, concentration, problem-solving, language, visual-spatial analysis, and emotional intelligence.

The whole app is based on the pair-matching game many of us have played with cards or on computers, but it builds upon this concept to challenge your mathematical skills, attention to detail, and ability to recognize associations. Through your **Apple Watch**, you can play a few small games each day to help keep your mental abilities in tune. The games include simple arithmetic that challenges you to remember numbers while you carry out calculations; determining whether two woords are antonyms or synonyms; finding matching figures in a group; or completing a logical sequence of numbers.

You will receive reports allowing you to track your progress and highlight your strengths and weaknesses. You can play personalized games each day to target your specific weaknesses while still keeping you engaged and enjoying yourself.

CHAPTER 6: Tips and Tricks

General Tips and Tricks to Help You Get the Most Out of Your Apple Watch

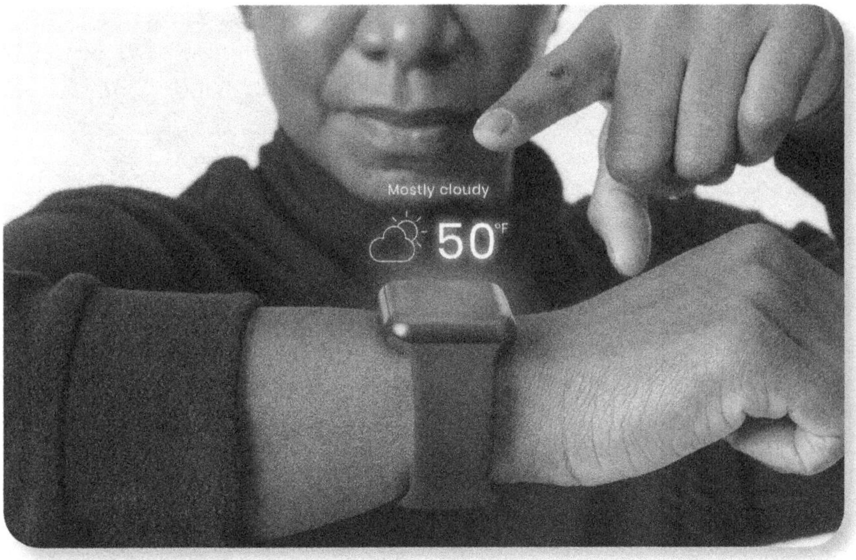

Create a Portrait Watch Face

Do you want to use one of your favorite pictures as the background for your Watch Face? All you need to do is go to the **Watch app** on your **iPhone** and then select **Face Gallery.** Scroll down until you see Portraits. Now you can select up to 24 photos you want to use for your watch face.

Once you have selected your photos, you can choose between some different styling options: **Classic**, **Modern**, or **Rounded face**, and then choose the **complication layout.** Add your complications to make sure your watch face meets all of your needs, and then when you are done, tap the **Add button** to save your watch face.

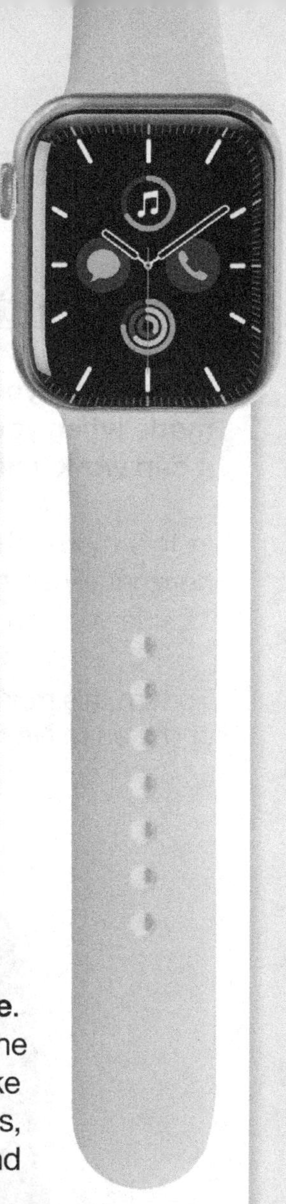

You can also create a watch face directly from the **Photos app** on your **iPhone**. In your album, find the photo you want to use and press the Share button at the bottom of the screen. Scroll down and select **Create Watch Face.** This will take you to a screen where you can select your layout, choose custom color options, and add complications. When you are done, tap Add to save the watch face and sync it with your **Apple Watch**.

To add a photo as your watch face directly from your **Apple Watch**, you will need to go to the **Photos app** on your watch. Here you will be able to see the photos that are synced from your **iPhone**.

Select the photo you want to use and tap the **share button**. You can choose customization options like the layout and colors, and add complications before adding your settings to the watch face.

Nightstand Mode

You can set your Apple Watch to bedside mode when you are not wearing it so that it can work just like a bedside clock.

In this mode, the watch face will be rotated horizontally so that when your watch is lying on its side you can see the time.

To turn this mode on or off, open the **Settings app** on your **Apple Watch**, scroll to **General**, and then to **Nightstand mode**, where you can toggle it on or off.

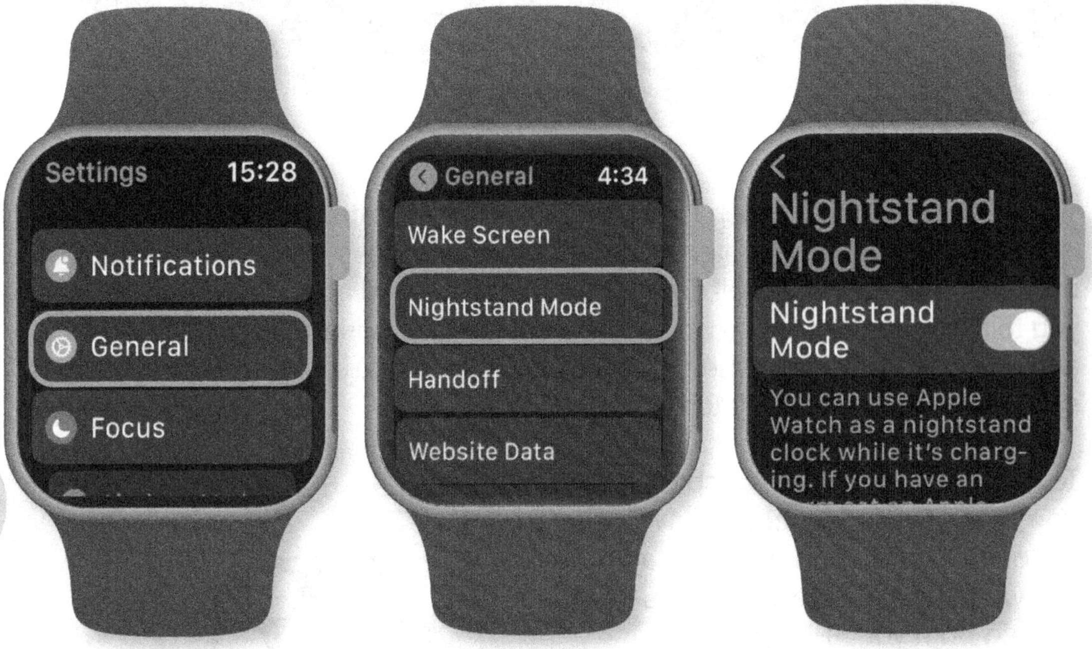

Clear All Notifications

If you have built up a long list of notifications and they are becomign cluttered and unmanageable, you can clear them all at the same time. All you need to do is swipe down on your watch face to view the notification list and then long-press anywhere on the screen. This will bring up a button giving you the option to Clear All.

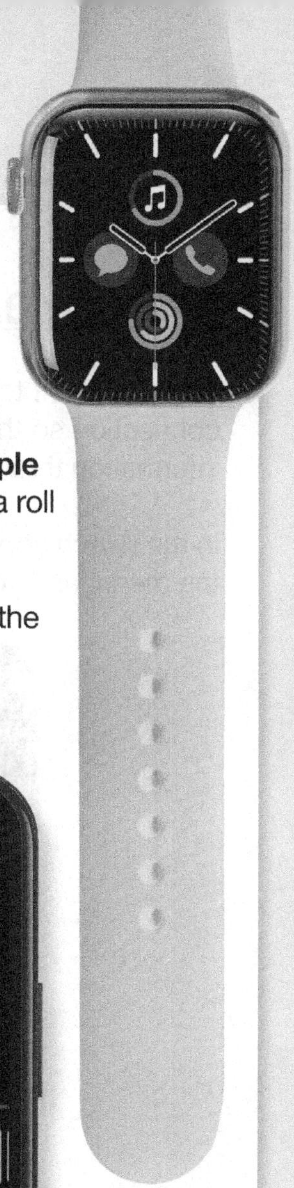

Take a Screenshot

You can take a screenshot of your Apple Watch display just like you would on your iPhone. All you need to do is press the **Digital Crown** and the side button at the same time. These screenshots will be saved on your **Apple Watch** and synced with your **iPhone**, where you can find them on the camera roll in your **Photos app**.

You may need to enable this feature on the **Watch app** on your **iPhone**. In the **General settings**, scroll to **Enable Screenshots** and toggle them on or off.

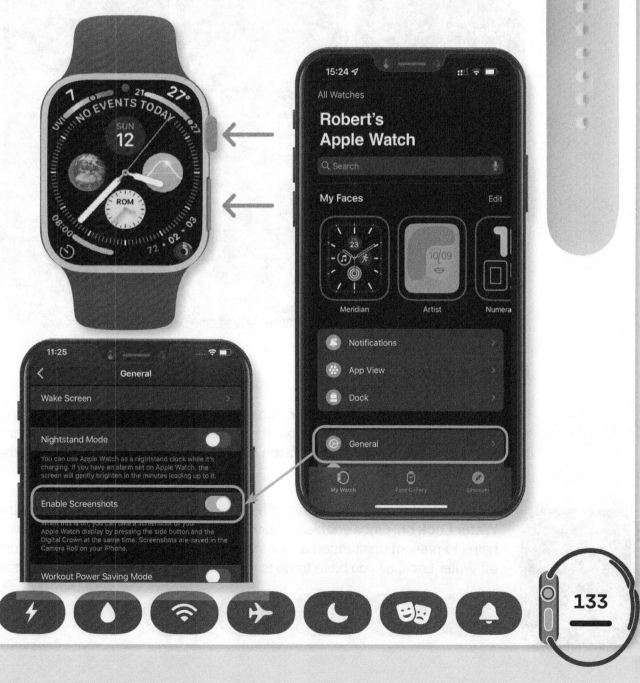

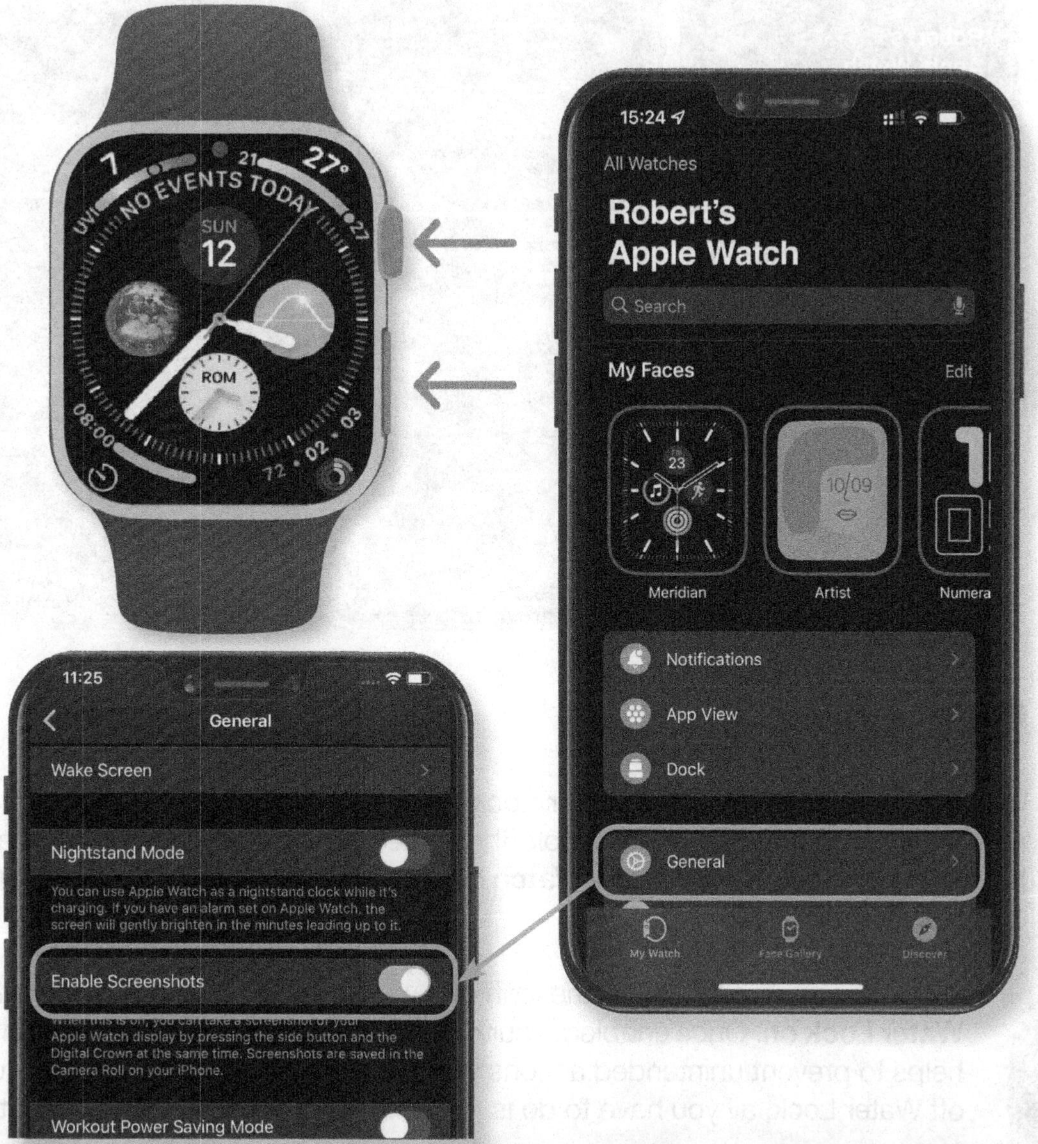

See Your Data Usage

You may want to keep an eye on your **data usage** if you have an **Apple Watch** with a cellular connection so that you can manage your monthly plan. Unfortunately, you can only view this information through the **Watch app** on your **iPhone**.

In the Watch app, tap the **My Watch tab** at the bottom of the screen. Then select **Cellular** from the menu, and you will be able to see important information about your data usage.

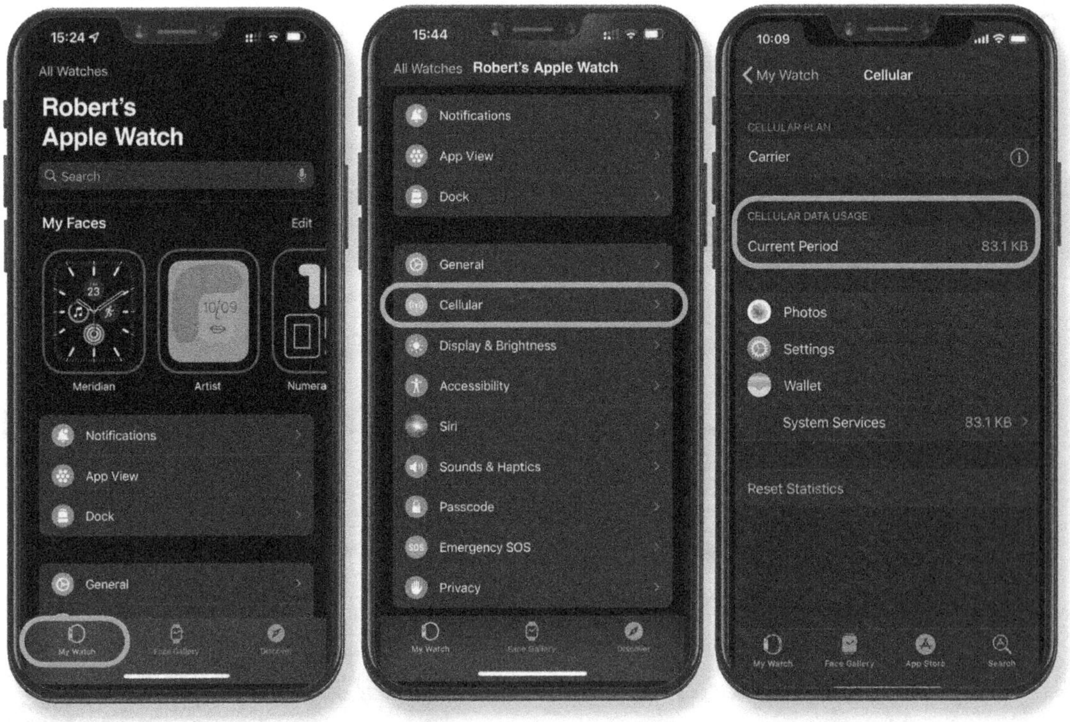

Eject Water

We have already covered the Water Lock feature on your **Apple Watch**, but to refresh your memory, you can enable the Water Lock feature by touching and holding the bottom of your **Apple Watch** display and then swiping up to view the **Control Center.**

Here you can scroll down to the icon of a water droplet and tap it to turn the **Water Lock on**. Once enabled, your display will not respond to touch, which helps to prevent unintended actions while you are busy in the water. To turn off Water Lock, all you have to do is rotate the Digital Crown in any direction

until you see the Unlock alert. Your **Apple Watch** will also play a series of tones out of its speaker to help clear away any water that remains.

Set the Time Ahead

If you are someone that hates being late or you are often late, you can set your watch a few minutes ahead to help you be punctual.

In the **Settings app** on your **Apple Watch**, scroll to **Clock**, and there you will be able to set your watch ahead or behind by up to 59 minutes.

This change won't affect your alarms, notifications, or world clock, but it can help you with your time management by giving you a little bit of leeway.

Share Your Location in a Message

Though the **Messages app** on your **Apple Watch** does have limited functionality, you can still communicate quite effectively using the default responses or voice-to-text.

You can also send your location to one of your contacts using Force Touch. In the message dialog, force touch the screen by holding and pressing harder than usual.

This will bring up a menu with additional options such as Reply, Details, Send Location, or Choose Language.

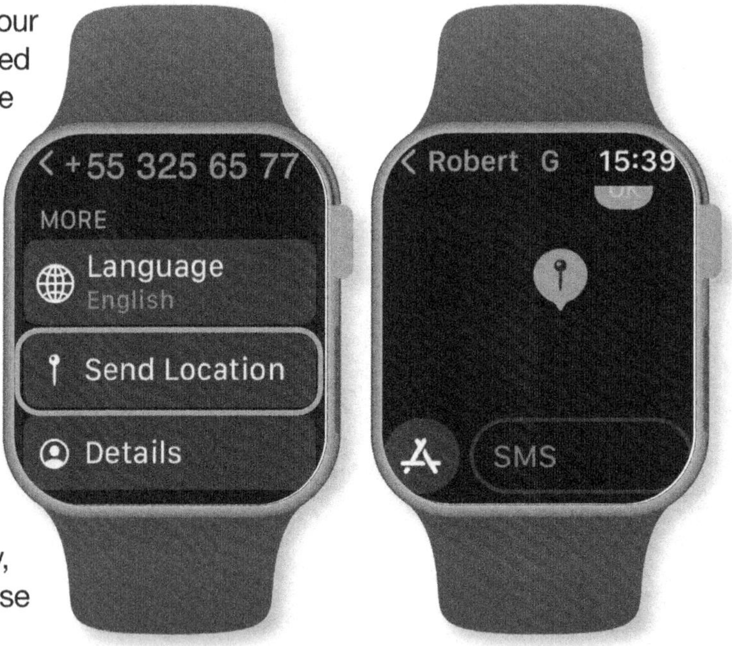

Tap the **Send Location button** to send your contact a **GPS** pin with your current location.

Hold a Call on Your Apple Watch

Even though you can receive calls on your **Apple Watch**, you may not always want to. If you are in the bathroom while someone calls, for example, you can tap the **Answer on iPhone button**, which will place the call on hold until you can reach your **iPhone** instead.

The person on the other side of the line will hear a repeating hold tone to let them know you are busy at the moment and will answer them shortly.

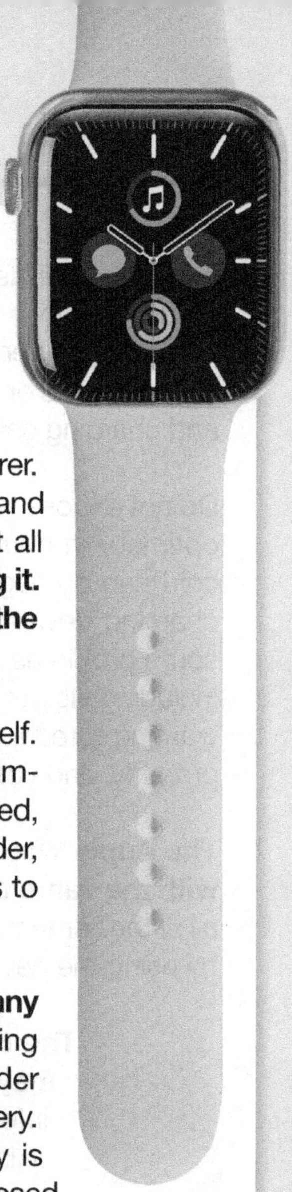

Important Information

The mishandling of your **Apple Watch** can result in some safety risks, including electric shock, fire, injury, or damage to the device. It is essential to always carefully follow the instructions provided in this guide and by the manufacturer. Though the **Apple Watch** is designed to endure various environments and situations, you should avoid dropping, burning, puncturing, or crushing it at all costs. **If your Apple Watch does become damaged, you should stop using it. This includes a cracked case or screen, visible liquid or droplets inside the case or screen, or a damaged band.**

It is strongly advised that you do not try to repair your **Apple Watch** by yourself. This can result in further damage to the unit, a loss of water resistance and swim-proof features, and you may become injured. If your device needs to be repaired, you will need to contact Apple or your nearest Apple Authorized Service Provider, who will be able to advise if your device can be repaired or whether it needs to be replaced.

Do not attempt to replace the battery in your device by yourself under any circumstances. You may damage the battery, which can result in overheating and potential explosions that can injure you. Only an authorized service provider will have the necessary tools and knowledge to replace the lithium-ion battery. You may be eligible to receive a temporary replacement while your battery is repaired. All lithium-ion batteries need to be appropriately handled and disposed of or recycled separately from typical household waste.

You should only charge your **Apple Watch** with the **Apple Watch** Magnetic Fast Charger to USB-C cable, the **Apple Watch** Magnetic Charging Cable, the MagSafe Duo Charger, or the **Apple Watch** Magnetic Charging Dock and other accredited Apple-branded compatible power units. There are also third-party power adapters that are compliant with USB 2.0 that can be used depending on your country's safety standards. If you choose to use any other type of charging device, you may risk damaging your **Apple Watch** device.

Do not use any damaged chargers or charging cables, and avoid using them when any moisture is present. This may result in a fire, electric shock, injury, or damage to the **Apple Watch** and your home. Make sure your adapters are always inserted properly and that you do not overload your plug systems.

Similarly, your device, charging cables, and chargers are sensitive to high temperatures. **Do not expose these items to high temperatures for prolonged**

periods. Your device batteries will become warm during charging, and this is to be expected, but be cautious if you feel them getting particularly hot and unplug them immediately. Make sure your power sources are free from clutter nad potential fire hazards. Do not sleep on your power cables or adapters or place them under a pillow or blanket. Avoid placing your chargers and charging cables near heaters or radiators.

Do not expose your **Apple Watch** to high temperatures either. Your device is designed to work optimally in normal ambient temperatures, and prolonged exposure to any extreme heat or cold can damage or shorten the battery life. Similarly, avoid exposing your **Apple Watch** or charging devices to excessively high humidity levels for prolonged periods. You can expect some problems if your **Apple Watch** is subjected to extreme temperatures or humidity levels, including slowed charging or inability to charge, a dimmed display, you may see a temperature warning screen, data transfer may be paused or delayed, some apps may close and not function properly, and you may not be able to use the cellular function if your model enables this.

The Apple Watch is designed to be a companion to your iPhone and should be treated with the same caution and awareness. When using your **Apple Watch**, you should observe all of the same rules that apply to a mobile device. Do not place yourself in dangerous situations by using the device while driving or operating other heavy machinery.

The Navigation features of your Apple Watch may be subject to change and may not be available in all areas. Your directions, maps, and location-based information may sometimes be unavailable, inaccurate, unreliable, or incomplete. It is your responsibility to ensure that the information provided by the device matches what you see in the real world and always observe real-world signage and warnings over those on your device. For example, the Maps app may not recognize one-way streets in all locations and may advise you to take a turn down one of these roads. You will need to find an alternate route that does not infringe upon laws and regulations. Always make sure to verify your device's directions against your own common sense.

Your Apple Watch and charging components will emit electromagnetic radiation that may interfere with medical devices such as implanted pacemakers or defribillators. You must consult with your physician if you have one of these devices and would like to use an **Apple Watch** to determine whether or not they will be compatible.

Remember that your Apple Watch is not a medical device and should not be used in place of a medical professional or their advice. The **Apple Watch** cannot be used to diagnose any type of medical condition, nor can it be used to cure, treat, prevent, or mitigate any disease or condition. Always

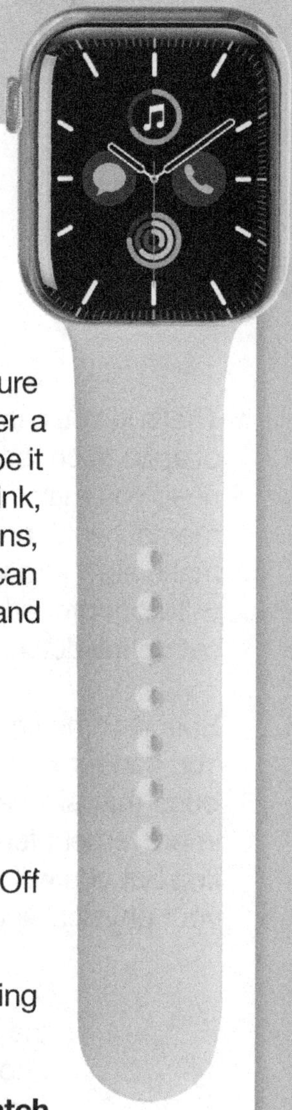

make sure to consult with your physician before beginning any new exercise program if you are at risk of any conditions such as seizures, blackouts, headaches, or eye strain, and if you ever feel any pain, dizziness, faintness, shortness of breath, or exhaustion.

To make your **Apple Watch** last and function as well as possible, make sure to carefully follow the charging instructions and keep it clean and dry. After a workout or sweaty day, make sure to remove the band from your wrist and wipe it down. Suppose your band or watch becomes dirty from sand, dirt, makeup, ink, foods, sweat, soapy water, chlorine, bleach, perfume, insect repellant, lotions, sunscreens, hair dye, solvents, or any other chemicals. In such a case, this can lead to irritation of your skin. It is important to make sure you clean your band regularly to prevent grime buildup.

The best way to clean your Apple Watch is to:

- **Turn your device** off by pressing and holding down the side button.
- When you see the power menu appear on the screen, slide the Power Off slider to the right.
- Remove the bands by depressing the band release button or unclipping the clasps.
- **Use a lint-free, nonabrasive cloth to wipe down the Apple Watch, including the front and the back.** You can also use a damp cloth if necessary.
- Do not clean your **Apple Watch** while it is charging.
- Allow your bands to air dry, and do not apply any heat.
- Avoid using any cleaning products like soaps or detergents.
- **Do not use compressed air to clean the device.**
- Depending on the model, your watch front is made from Ion-X glass or sapphire crystal, and these have a fingerprint-resistant coating that repels oil. This coating will diminish over time through normal use, and the use of any cleaning products or abrasive cloths will accelerate this process.
- Avoid using abrasive materials that may scratch the watch front.

CONCLUSION

That's it! You can now go out and use your **Apple Watch** with confidence. With a large selection of apps to choose from, you can make sure your device is personalized to meet each and every need you may have, from helping you to be more productive during the day to monitoring your mental health and alerting you if something looks wrong with your heart rate. It is important to make sure that you have enabled all of the health and emergency SOS features so that they will work properly when you need them most. Make sure to add your emergency contacts and set up fall detection.

Spend some time going through the App Store and playing around with a few different apps. You can remove an app at any time if you feel it is not good, doesn't meet your needs, or has bugs that still need to be worked out by the developers. Take advantage of some of the life improvement features like sleep, water, and fitness tracking. These may seem like a nuisance at first but you will come to appreciate them as you begin to notice how they can actually improve your physical and mental well-being.

On a final note, your premium device offers you only the best features and carefully curated content. You should also protect your device further by ensuring you have a passcode set and purchasing a protective case or screen cover so that it doesn't get damaged.

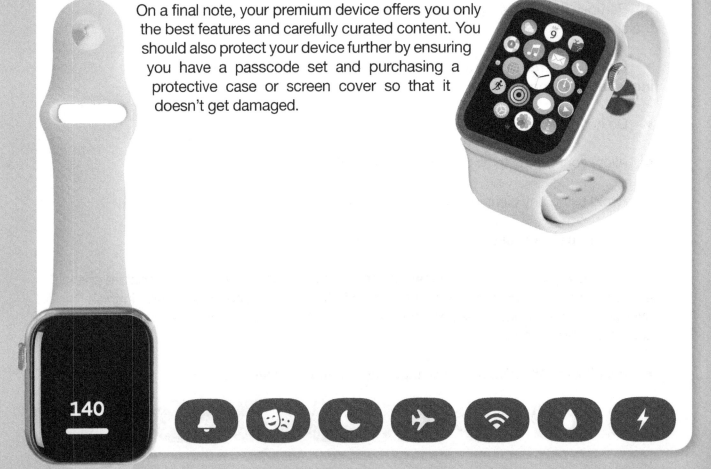

INDEX

SYMBOLS

A

B

C

T

Made in the USA
Monee, IL
30 September 2024

66859240R00083